HELLENISM AND CHRISTIANITY

HELLENISM AND CHRISTIANITY

BY

EDWYN BEVAN

HONORARY FELLOW OF NEW COLLEGE, OXFORD

Essay Index Reprint Series

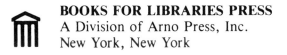

BOOKS FOR LIBRARIES PRESS
A Division of Arno Press, Inc.
New York, New York

First Published 1921
Reprinted 1967

LIBRARY OF CONGRESS CATALOG CARD NUMBER: 67-26714

PRINTED IN THE UNITED STATES OF AMERICA

PREFACE

THE essays composing this book were written at different times for different occasions. Yet I venture to believe that, put together in a single volume, they will present a mental unity—a single body of interests, observations, and ideas, which is one individual's reaction to the spectacle of the universe. In the history of mankind, during these last few thousand years, in which mankind has begun to have what may be called in the more special sense a history, the two predominant factors appear to be, (1) the rise of rationalist culture, first in the ancient Greek world and then again in modern European civilization, and (2) the entrance of the Christian life into the world process. In the first essay I have tried to show the significance of rationalist culture in its relation to Eastern forms of civilization, and correct what I believe to be some common misapprehensions. Perhaps some explanation is required why this essay in describing the civilization of the West says nothing about Christianity. This is not because I think Christianity an unimportant element in the life of mankind; it is because the modern West seems to me still for a large part to require conversion to Christianity. Such genuine Christianity as has existed in the West has no doubt exerted an incalculable influence in different

Hellenism and Christianity

degrees over the whole field, but when men contrast our modern Western civilization with Eastern civilizations, when they lay stress upon our standards of political life, our intellectual emancipation, our science, our mastery over the forces of Nature, they are pointing rather to the Hellenic, rationalist, factor in our civilization than to the Christian. It is that which constitutes, if I may so express it, the " Westernness of the West." I once heard a living politician, speaking on a platform, claim for Christianity, amongst other things, credit for the invention of lyddite shells. That seems to me a confusion.

The two following essays deal with the ancient Hellenism. Bacchylides raises the problem why rationalist culture in its first Hellenic embodiment met with an arrest. In the Greek Anthology, of which the third essay treats, there is brought before us an image of the Greek mind in its later literary activities, and we are left listening to the ancient voice calling out of the perished centuries its ever-recurrent burden, " Let us eat and drink and follow our light loves, for to-morrow we die."

In the next two essays we look at the first entrance of the Christian life into this world which fears death, the distinctive Christian idea of the Redeemer. Then we pass to the time when the old paganism is on the point of extinction and the new world of medieval Christianity about to be born, to the great typical figure of Augustine on the threshold of the two ages. In the eighth and ninth essays some questions of moral value connected with the Christian view of life are discussed. If the essays hitherto have looked backwards along the human track through time and tried to discover the significance of

Preface

Christianity by glancing at some of the things that went before it, or that have accompanied it up to the present, the tenth and eleventh essays consider the question whither the whole process is tending, since our idea of the significance of any factor in the world movement must be determined as much by our forecast of what it is leading to as by our view of its antecedents. Since the essay on Human Progress was written two notable contributions have been made to the discussion of this question, Professor Bury's book on "The Idea of Progress" and the Romanes Lecture given in 1920 by the Dean of St. Paul's. My more discursive treatment of the subject in this essay, however, trenches so little upon theirs, that what I wrote some years ago may still contribute something of an individual character. The last two essays have to do with the relations between Christianity and the rationalist element in our culture and try to determine what the truth is with regard to the conflict supposed to exist between them and the position of Christianity to-day after four centuries of growing rationalism have shaken and sifted the thoughts of men.

The essay entitled "The Religion of Cheerfulness," the essay on "Human Progress," and that on "The Problem of Eschatology," are published now for the first time. "The First Contact of Christianity and Paganism" appeared in the *Quarterly Review*, the first and last essays in the *Nineteenth Century and After*, "Dirt" in the *Contemporary Review*, "The Gnostic Redeemer" in the *Hibbert Journal*, "Between Two Worlds" and "Reason and Dogma" in *The Quest*, "Bacchylides," "The Greek Anthology" and "The

Hellenism and Christianity

Prophet of Personality " in the Literary Supplement of *The Times*. Grateful acknowledgement is due to the editors and publishers of these several periodicals who have given permission for the essays enumerated to be republished as constituents of this book.

September, 1921.

CONTENTS

Hellenism and Christianity

I

THE EAST AND THE WEST

EVEN people who have given little thought to a Philosophy of History are attracted by those large generalizations that promise to bring some consistency and meaning into the strange multifarious drama unrolling itself upon this planet, since the creature known to naturalists as *Homo Sapiens* became a fact of the universe. There are few men but in a dim way and at odd moments are curious to understand something of the vaster forces and currents on which they find themselves carried, and all the men of their generation carried, into unknown gulfs of time. Behind the individual lives which flicker and vanish, there seem to be greater permanent entities engaged in secular conflict—races, types, ideas, through all the pains and passions of men working out their transcendent destinies. That is one of the reasons why such phrases as that which sets the East against the West, or Asia against Europe, have such enormous popular appeal. They have but to be uttered, and immediately the modern Englishman, involved in such problematic relations to-day with the peoples of Asia, feels himself the representative of an eternal principle. Yes, he sees it all. Behind him, and all other Englishmen, there is a great Something, an abiding character, something which he calls the "West"; behind all the congeries of alien peoples there is another great Something, the "East." These two have been enacting their mutual rôles all through the ages. The present situation between them is merely a moment in that unending interplay.

The instinct which makes us desire such large generalizations, key-words to bring light and order into the bewildering complexity of the world, is no doubt a sound one. That the desire satisfies itself in an extraordinarily haphazard and undiscriminating fashion is, unfortunately, also true. About "the East" and "the West," for instance, one must recognize that a dreadful amount of nonsense has been talked and written. You may make almost any statement you like about the "Oriental mind," and be sure of producing your effect.

To begin with, it has always appeared to me an unfortunate usage, which describes the contrast before us by the points of the compass, as East and West, or by continents, as Asia and Europe. It is true, of course, that the type of civilization which is denoted by the term "Western" or "European" is characteristic of Europe *to-day*, and that the Asiatic peoples, except in so far as they have assimilated elements from the West, agree in the negative quality of not possessing the peculiar marks of our modern civilization. That is undeniable. Why the terms appear to me unfortunate and misleading is that the contrast we see to-day is not merely between peoples of different blood and habitation, but between

The East and the West

peoples at different stages of development. Qualities which are ascribed with an unreflecting readiness to the "Oriental" often turn out on inspection to be not in the least peculiar to the East, but qualities universal among peoples at the more primitive stage. Many of them might have been discovered just as much in medieval Europe. The Crusaders would find it much easier to enter into the feelings of many Oriental peoples to-day than into those of their own descendants in France or Germany. The West for a great part of its history has not been "Western." On the other hand, the differences between Oriental peoples themselves are so great as to make the "East" a generalization too wide and vague to be of real service. One has only to mark the result when popular writers set out with it—the marvellous statements that are constantly given forth as to the "Oriental" mind.

What is meant by "Western civilization" is, in fact, the product of a peculiar development which has taken place in the European branch of the human family during the last four or five centuries—a brief enough span of time compared with the four or five millenniums which separate us from the builders of the Pyramids, or the unnumbered millenniums which separate us from Palæolithic man. This civilization, it is true, has had its antecedents in the West; it resumes a development which took place about the shores of the Mediterranean from some 2,600 to some 1,600 years ago. It is strictly continuous with the classical civilization of Greece and Rome—in a real sense its child. We may therefore truly regard the Hellenistic and Roman dominion in the East as workings of the same principle which is embodied in our dominion upon

Hellenism and Christianity

a somewhat similar field. We may with Lord Cromer look upon those earlier ventures as experiments which may throw some light upon our own. There is justification for classing the three experiments, the Hellenistic (Macedonian), the Roman, the modern, together as a consecutive story of " European rule." If, indeed, we could be sure that " European " would always be taken in a sense restricting it to the Europe of classical times and Europe since the Renaissance, there would be no harm in using it as the distinctive way of describing our civilization. Unfortunately, in popular use it is almost certain to carry with it the implication that this civilization is a permanent, inalienable characteristic of the races who live between certain longitudes.

We want some convenient way of describing it; for while the " East " stands for an indefinite medley of varying traditions, the modern civilization of Europe is certainly a unity. To call it " modern " simply would emphasize its recent origin, its difference from the older, more stationary, societies of Asia, but would hardly fix its character with any particularity. We might call it Hellenistic, if we gave a sufficiently large meaning to that word. For if the ancient classical culture and European culture since the Renaissance are phases in the manifestation of a single principle, we want some name which would include them both, and yet not, like " European," have too wide a denotation. Perhaps the best way would be to speak of this type of culture as Rationalistic Civilization. That would describe it by an essential characteristic of its vital principle, and beg no questions as to its being confined to this or that set of people or quarter of the globe. What in the last resort gave its peculiar note to Hellenism as against all that existed outside it? Surely just the singular development of those mental faculties, which we associate with rationalism, the critical intellect, the bent to submit traditions and belief to logical examination, the desire to get the values of things in their real proportions. It was because the Greeks could stand off from established custom, and ask the reason Why, that they could make political progress; because they could feel the inadequacy of ancestral mythology and ask what the world was really made of, that they could lay the foundations of rational science. It was fundamentally the same mental quality which kept their Art for all its idealism so sane, so closely in touch with Nature, which eliminated instinctively the dispro-portionate, the monstrous. The answers which the old Greeks worked out to their questions may not satisfy us to-day; the important thing is that they began putting these questions in this way at all. If our thoughts have been carried further, it was they who began the train of thought. All the development of knowledge, of command over the forces of Nature, of purposeful order, which is meant by the term "Western Civilization" to-day, has had for its moving principle a rationalism whose origin is to be found in the Greek city-states.

On the other hand, I do not think that we need any one term for covering what is understood by the "East." It is just the classing of this heterogeneous mass together which has led to all the muddle. The question "What has been, or will be, the effect of Rationalistic Civiliza-tion upon the East?" is really a confused one, and could be replaced advantageously by questions which have some meaning, "What will be the effect of Rationalistic

Hellenism and Christianity

Civilization upon India? upon Japan? upon China? upon Persia? upon the Turks?" Of course it is easy to see how the Western man comes to class all these peoples together. It is some shock, I suppose, to the more ingenuous traveller from the West to find standards of value or conceptions which are a part of his inheritance not acknowledged by, let us say, the Turks. If he continues his travels to Persia, the shock is repeated. Let him go on to India; the same thing here! The same in China! in Japan! The negative agreement among all these peoples in rejecting what are special characteristics of the West staggers him so that he hardly notices all their positive differences. Out of this negative agreement he creates the imaginary "Oriental." It does not occur to him to ask whether he would not experience a similar shock, if he travelled back in time, among the people of his own land. Or in many cases he may not even superficially become acquainted with more than one corner of Asia. Then his "Oriental" tends to be the inhabitant of that corner generalized and extended over the continent. A writer in the *Edinburgh Review* for October 1910 states, on the authority of Max Müller, that "the sentiment of love for Nature and the feeling for natural beauty have in India no existence" (!) And he goes on to say : "The slight knowledge of such matters which three years passed among the Tamil coolies and Cingalese villagers of Ceylon may be expected to confer would certainly incline the present writer to the same conclusion. None of the common daily signs, as the flowers of a cottage garden, or plants even in slum windows, which testify in the West to the inarticulate deep feeling for Nature which prevails, belong to the life of India.

The East and the West

We never saw a native evince the slightest sign of a recognition of natural beauty, and even the instinctive delight of children which we associate with posies and daisy-chains seems to form no part of the experience of an Indian childhood." "All matter," this writer says, "the outer semblances of Nature equally with the form of man, is in Eastern thought a delusion. The Wordsworthian idea of whispers of the infinite conveyed by mountains and mists is Western, not Eastern." Here is just an instance of how the unfortunate dragging in of "East" and "West" vitiates observations which, in reference to their own limited sphere may be shrewd and interesting. Granting that sensibility to the beauty of flowers and mountains and mists is a quality not strongly developed among Tamil coolies, why call this characteristic "Eastern"? One has but to look a little further East, to Japan, to see a people whose passion for natural beauty, for flowers and mountains and mists, makes the ordinary European feeling for such things seem cold. Probably many observers, for whom "the East" means Japan, would tell you that a deep feeling for the significance of natural beauty was just one of the characteristics which distinguished "the Oriental" from his prosaic brother of the West.[1]

[1] As a matter of fact, since I wrote the above, I have heard Dr. Rabindranath Tagore maintain in a lecture that the Wordsworthian love of Nature was so essentially Indian that its appearance in the West was to be explained by the influence of Indian thought then beginning to affect Europe. We have really to do here, I believe, with something which is neither Western nor Eastern, but broadly human. The assertion that the love for Nature and the feeling for natural beauty have in India no existence seems so preposterous that one has a difficulty in supposing Max Müller, who certainly was acquainted with Sakuntala, to have been

Hellenism and Christianity

Having created his generalized " Oriental," the popular theory goes on to declare that between " East " and " West " there is a great gulf fixed, an eternal distinction.

Here, again, it seems to me we touch a confusion which sets discussion in this field at cross purposes. There will always be a *difference*, mental as well as physical, between the natives of England and the natives of India, for example. No sane person would wish to deny that. But the popular theory asserts a great deal more : it asserts that the " West " can have no real or permanent influence upon the " East." That is the assertion I mean to traverse. When we say that one person has " influence " upon another, or one people upon another, we mean simply that in some respect the subsequent life of the person or people influenced is different from what it would otherwise have been, different in the way of being more or less assimilated to the other personality, or the other national type. We do not mean that all distinction between the two persons or peoples is obliterated. If I observed, for instance, that Mr. Chesterton had been " influenced " by Robert Browning, I should not mean that, if Mr. Chesterton came into the room, you could defy me to tell whether it was Mr. Chesterton or Browning come to life again. Yet one has but to assert that the civilization of England is influencing an Eastern people, and some one will jump up to refute you by pointing out that this or that original point of difference between the two peoples subsists still. " So

correctly quoted by the writer in the *Edinburgh Review*. On the other hand, to suppose Indian or Oriental influence, wherever men in any part of the world have found the divine revealed in the beauty of Nature, would also seem to me preposterous.

much for your boasted influence ! " It seems as if there were some general inability in the popular mind to conceive anything between the two extremes. It must be all or nothing. Either the influence of our civilization must be nil, or it must efface every vestige of distinction ; either it must make India an exact duplicate of England, or our government must be a momentary phantom which will vanish and leave not a trace behind.

To hold the latter view is felt apparently by many people to be a sign of superior penetration, or of exaltation above the crude hopes of the multitude, of a sad, far-seeing wisdom. If you question it you are credited with a naïve belief in the other alternative, a belief that India is being transformed, or is practically transformed, into a country indistinguishable from Europe. The grounds upon which the negative view is held are either (1) historical, the alleged fact that the Greek and Roman influence upon the East was evanescent, or (2) the experi- ence of modern observers, which is supposed to show that all Western influence to-day is skin-deep. To deal first with the historical argument, it seems at first sight plain enough. Asia Minor and Syria were once upon a time under Hellenistic rule (Macedonian and Roman —Rome in the East acted as a Hellenizing, rather than as a Latinizing, power) ; to-day Asia Minor and Syria are Mohammedan and beyond the pale of Western culture. There you are—Q.E.D. Unfortunately, this argument loses somewhat in cogency if the facts are looked into more precisely. Supposing the peoples of Asia Minor and Syria had been left after some centuries of Hellenistic rule to take their own way, and had then reverted to earlier types, rejecting the alien plant of Hellenism—

Hellenism and Christianity

then, I admit, we should have some reason for saying that the experiment had tended to show an incompatibility of Hellenistic culture with that particular Asiatic soil. But this is not what happened. The peoples of Asia Minor and Syria were not left to take their own way. They were conquered and overrun by other peoples coming in from regions almost untouched by Hellenistic influence. If my garden has been swept by a flood and the plants I was trying to rear destroyed, it would hardly be fair to argue from their disappearance a native unfriendliness of the soil. But the noteworthy thing in this case is that Hellenism was not destroyed. " When, after several centuries," says another article in the *Edinburgh Review*, " the Byzantine power in the East was overthrown by the Mohammedan conquests, it was succeeded by a government which despised and rejected the sciences, philosophies, and letters of the West."

Now, as to this statement, I can only say that it seems to me diametrically opposed to the facts of history. Probably the story (long recognized as mythical) of the burning of the Alexandrian library by Caliph Omar has caused the popular imagination to conceive of the Mohammedan conquerors as uncompromising enemies of Hellenistic culture. The original Arab followers of the Prophet did no doubt stand outside its sphere of influence, no less than the Goths and Franks who came down upon the Mediterranean lands from the North. But just as the Northern barbarians, when they had once settled upon the lands of the old civilization, began to absorb elements (scanty enough for many centuries) of the classical tradition, so the Mohammedans, when they had created great settled kingdoms upon the old territory

The East and the West

of the Greco-Roman Empire, began to absorb the ration·
alistic lore of the conquered. A great amount of the
Greek learning was still current, and current largely
throughout the Syriac-speaking provinces in native
versions, when the Mohammedan conquerors entered
into possession, and through the medium of Syriac all
this passed as a substantial constituent into the new
Arabic culture. This is not an obscure conjecture. It is
an acknowledged fact standing out clearly in the history
of Arabic literature [1] The Mohammedan civilization
knew a science of grammar; it was based openly upon
the logic of Aristotle. There is no question as to the
Hellenistic origin of Arabic geography, Arabic geometry,
Arabic astronomy, Arabic medicine. One would think
that when we got to Mohammedan mysticism, to the
religious philosophy of the Sufis, we ought, according to
the popular theory, to have something purely " Oriental."
Unfortunately, the European scholars seem agreed in
finding here a strong trace of Neo-Platonic influence.
It is fair to say that modern Mohammedan scholars
claim an independent origin for Sufism. For our purposes
we need not trouble about the settlement of the controversy: the fact that the question can be raised at all
proves so striking an affinity between Sufism and Neo-
Platonism as to show the futility of the popular theory
which draws a hard and fast line between " Oriental
Mysticism " and " Western Materialism." So far, then,
from its being true that Hellenism was a plant which
could only flourish among natives of Europe, there was

[1] One may consult the standard histories, Brockelmann's " Ges-
chichte der Arabischen Literatur," or Professor Nicholson's
" Literary History of the Arabs."

Hellenism and Christianity

a time when Aristotle, returning to the world, would have found his name more honoured and his thoughts better understood in Bagdad and Samarkand than in Athens and Rome.

I know what is answered : " Look at Bagdad and Samarkand to-day ; where is their Hellenism now ? " Well, it is not anything very imposing, one must admit. So far indeed as the tradition of Mohammedan learning is still cultivated there, something of what was learnt in the great days of Islam survives. When the native Persian doctor appeals to the authority of Pocrat, the European traveller may not detect any Western influence, but Pocrat is the old Greek Hippocrates for all that. Yet what survives of Hellenism is, there is no denying, a very starved and shrunken growth. Now, if we found in the Mohammedan world to-day a flourishing culture in which the non-Hellenic elements had grown strong at the expense of the Hellenic, then we might argue from the decline of these latter that they were essentially incompatible with the " Oriental mind." But what we really find is that Mohammedan culture as a whole has decayed during the last five centuries. The five centuries which in Europe have witnessed the development of this wonderful new thing, this Rationalistic Civilization, have been for the Mohammedan East centuries of waning force and diminishing intellectual activity. The Nearer East, as it was seen by European travellers in the nineteenth century, was a ruin. Its whole intellectual life was feeble, not only as compared with that of modern Europe, but as compared with that of its own golden prime. The Hellenic elements in Mohammedan culture had decayed along with all the rest. When we ask the reason of this

The East and the West

decline, we are asking a question possibly susceptible of many answers. Nothing is harder to mark with precision than the causes at work in the decay of anything so complex as a great society. Probably, however, one main cause to which the downfall of the Mohammedan East was due may be discerned in its greater exposure to barbarian invasion and infiltration from Central Asia. Ancient civilization, from the earliest times to which the ken of history can reach, was continually in danger of being swamped by invasion from the vast barbarian world outside. Throughout the history of Egypt, of Babylonia, of Greece, of Rome, the irruption of barbarian hordes comes at intervals as a recurring episode, disturbing and terrifying. And these movements of the barbarian mass usually took their start from Central Asia. When the Hyksos burst into Egypt, when Kimmerians and Scythians devastated Asia Minor, when the Gallic hordes swept down upon Italy and Greece, when Goths and Vandals submerged the Roman Empire, all these peoples were being pushed by other tribes from behind, and it was from somewhere in Central Asia that the original push on each occasion seems to have begun. Against the enormous mass of barbarism bearing down upon it from this quarter, ancient civilization waged a secular war, an ultimately losing war. It beat back wave upon wave. Rome extended its own language, its own culture, over the barbarians of Gaul and Spain. But in the end the mass was too large for it to subdue or penetrate. It was submerged by the invaders from the North, and Europe had its " Dark Ages." Slowly from under the mass the tradition of the old rationalistic culture began to work upwards again, just as the same tradition worked, as we

Hellenism and Christianity

have seen, in the Nearer East among the Mohammedan invaders. And in the Middle Ages, as we have seen, it was in the East rather than in the West that it seemed to be reviving most fully. Meanwhile a great change was taking place on the globe ; Central Asia, the volcano which had thrown out for ages these streams of barbarian humanity, was becoming extinct. The region was drying up. Its last eruption was the discharge of Mongolian peoples, Turks and Moghals, whose forward movement was still vigorous in the fifteenth century. But it was the last wave, and Europe, farther from the centre of disturbance, was spared at the critical moment, when its intellectual life was on the point of reviving. It was only at one corner that it suffered loss, the last remains of the Byzantine Empire, with the Imperial City itself, being overwhelmed by the Ottoman Turks. But Europe as a whole escaped, and the five wonderful centuries followed. The Mohammedan culture of the East, on the other hand, was ruined past recovery by the tide of invasion from Central Asia. If the old tradition has never ceased, if even the Turks learnt something from the people whom they conquered, the Mohammedan East has been decrepit, without the power of fresh intellectual production during these centuries, and lands which were great and splendid under Harun-al-Rashid have gone to wilderness.

What wonder that in those circumstances the Hellenistic tradition resumed in Europe with such incalculable result at the Renaissance should have remained in the East a scanty and sterile survival ? And what sense is there in concluding from that fact a native incapacity of " the Oriental " ? To go back to our simile of the garden, if I find that in the part of my garden swept by the flood

The East and the West

the plants I introduced no less than the native growths are in a sorry way, what can I conclude from that as to the capacities of the soil ?

The historical argument, then, that " Asia has never been permanently influenced by Europe," looks rather foolish in the light of real history. But quite apart from the actual issue of the Hellenistic experiment, the notion that the future is likely to be a mere repetition of the past seems to me based upon an altogether false view of the course of the world. I believe we are entering upon a phase unlike anything that has ever been before. We may, I think, distinguish a succession of epochs in human history, each characterized by an advance in the communication of thought, and hence a possibility of larger co-operation. The facts confronting the most primitive groups of human beings demanded an amount of co-operation impossible without Speech, but with Speech alone there obviously cannot be co-operation over a wide field or consistency of effort along a series of generations. It was not till Speech was supplemented by Writing that the more complex tasks of the civilized peoples of antiquity could be attempted ; whether the civilization was that of a monarchical state like Egypt, Persia, and the Roman Empire, or that of city-states like the Greek Republics, it was a system impossible without Writing. When the Modern World was ushered in at the Renaissance, Writing was again supplemented by Printing, and now over fields as large as the monarchies of antiquity there was a possibility of co-operation resembling, although one cannot quite say equalling in closeness, that which had marked the old city-states. Without Printing, the European States of which

Hellenism and Christianity

" Western " civilization is the product, would have been impossible. But within the last two or three generations the possibilities of communication have again been enormously extended by the railway, the steamer, the telegraph, the telephone. We are entering upon the Telephonic Era. May we not expect that now co-operation for yet greater tasks between much larger groups of the human family will follow? The peoples of the world have never been brought so close together before ; all generalizations drawn from the past as to what is possible or not in the way of transmission of influence would anyway come short if applied to the new conditions of the time to come.

But in another way also the conditions under which civilization exists to-day are different from those prevailing in antiquity. Then, as we have seen, civilization lived under the perpetual menace of the barbarian world beyond its borders. There is now no similar danger. This is not only due to the depopulation of Central Asia and the spread of civilization or semi-civilization over large tracts once in outer barbarian darkness, but it is mainly due to the fact that a huge superiority of material power is attached to modern Rationalistic Civilization, a superiority which the civilizations of antiquity did not possess.

The superiority given by its discipline to the civilized army of antiquity over the barbarian was very much less than that given to the civilization of to-day by its command of scientific instruments. Not that the scientific instruments by themselves would suffice, but the vast combinations in strategy which they render possible can only be carried out by minds trained in the school of

The East and the West

Rationalistic Civilization. War still requires the old qualities of physical courage and energy and endurance —a raw material of brute and dogged hardihood is still invaluable—but these things avail less than ever apart from the fine directing brain. Civilization can no longer be overthrown by any barbarian onset. The inalienable superiority in material power attaches, of course, to Rationalistic Civilization itself, not to any race at present dominant. That the European *races* might be threatened by the Chinese, for instance, is quite conceivable, but only if the Chinese first recast their ancient civilization along the lines of European progress. Their victory would then be the victory of the more civilized people, and however galling to the racial pride of our descendants, might serve the interests of humanity. Already one Eastern people has had the better in an encounter with a European Power, but it was an Eastern people who had learnt from European instructors the means of victory. The *race* which won was Eastern ; the *principles* which won were of the West.

The other line of argument directed to disproving the influence of " Western " civilization upon " Orientals " is based upon the alleged experience of modern observers. Of course, nobody can deny the fact that in all civilized countries of Asia there is a class of men who have to all appearance become assimilated in greater or less degree to educated men of the West. It is not denied that there are numbers of individuals of Eastern origin whose knowledge of Western literature or Western science is superior to that of the vast majority of Westerns with whom they come in contact. But lest we should build too much upon this appearance, two considerations are urged by those who wish to keep up the popular theory of the "Oriental." First we are bid to take note that these educated men form only a very small fraction of their respective peoples. This is no doubt true, and there may be people who need to be reminded of it. There may be people who, having met in Europe some cultivated Indian or Japanese, imagine that all Indians or Japanese are like that, and would wish our public action to be founded on that supposition. But I can hardly believe that this opinion needs to be seriously taken account of. The fact, indeed, that the class imbued with Western education is a small minority is indubitable. The question is, What consequences, theoretical and practical, are to be drawn from this fact? Perhaps we shall be told that if all further influence from Rationalistic Civilization in the West ceased henceforward, the small class in question left isolated would not be able to hold its own against the mass of its own countrymen, that "Western" culture would disappear in a few generations. One need not, I think, deny that this is possible, though it seems to me, in view of the vitality of Hellenism under adverse conditions, exceedingly doubtful. Only the "if" is an absurd one; so long as Rationalistic Civilization exists in Europe its influence upon the rest of the world must go on. If it be contended that the class educated in the Western sense can never be large enough to dominate their respective countries, it seems to me that the assertion goes beyond anything that we have a right to say. And to be candid, one must also acknowledge that the really educated class is still in a minority in Europe. It is ridiculous to talk as if the rationalistic culture we describe as "Western" had permeated all classes of society here or anywhere else. In Europe itself there is a great mass of primitive barbarism kept under control by the civilized part of the community. It seems to me questionable whether the difference is very great between the peasantry of India or China and the peasantry in the south of Europe. If the Indian peasant is capable of believing that the Government poisons the wells, and the Chinese peasant of believing that Europeans capture children to extract photographic chemicals from their corpses, the peasantry in the south of France were capable some years ago of believing that Queen Victoria owed the singular vigour of her latter years to a secret consumption of the blood of babies. In England, no doubt, popular education has become too extensive to allow even the poorest class to entertain notions quite of that quality, but one has to go no further than to the sister island to find a peasantry capable apparently of believing that their priests can turn them into rats. It is true that the relative size and influence of the rationalistically educated class is much greater in Europe to-day than in India or China, but there is, I think, nothing to show that the proportion prevailing to-day is immutably fixed, or that rationalistic education may not, even within the next few generations, have an enormous extension in Asia.

In the second place, it is urged that the class itself which purports to have assimilated " Western " education is not really " Western " at heart ; that the " Western " culture is a " veneer " which is easily thrown off under native influences. Here we have plainly something very hard to prove, since it is a question of going below appearances, and much depends upon those personal intuitions about which one cannot argue. Personally, I have no sort of doubt that there are many men of Eastern race whose assimilation of modern European culture has been thoroughly genuine and vital. To any one who has come into close relation with some of these, the suggestion of any doubt upon this head would be as absurd as it would be in the case of any of his European friends. Yet we cannot, perhaps, meet the popular allegation unless we first recognize that there is a truth behind it which gives it whatever force it has, and then determine just what that truth is. In the first place there are, no doubt, persons of whom it is absolutely true. My Indian friends would, I think, readily admit that there were a certain number of their countrymen who had acquired the phrases of Western culture without acquiring much else. That this should be so was inevitable. When a system of thought and life passes from one people to another it is obvious that it does not pass in a single block, to be taken or rejected whole. It is plain that some parts of it are much more easily transmissible than others, and that among the most easily transmissible parts are phrases and catchwords. The transmission of intellectual habits is harder, and that of moral much harder still. Under these conditions, what else could take place except that the more easily transmissible parts should in many quarters outstrip the less transmissible, that there should be all degrees of imperfect assimilation between the fullest apprehension and total unreceptiveness. The fluent and superficial Oriental is a type which exists, and observers who judge things grossly and in the lump, who deal in generalizations about the "Oriental," take him for representative, just as certain unpleasing types of Englishmen are apt to be taken as representatives by those who do not love us.

When old residents in the East warn us against being deceived by appearances in the case of men of Eastern blood and Western education, their hardened scepticism seems to me to have two causes psychologically. One is that long acquaintance with the East at close quarters no doubt tends to make a man less liable to be deceived by a merely outward show of European culture. Old residents of this kind are probably inclined to give a disproportionate value to length of residence as compared with the natural gift of intelligence and sympathy. There are men on whom no length of residence in any country could confer the power of seeing below the surface, and there are men who almost at the first moment divine and understand. But we may grant, I think, to the old resident that, other things being equal, daily dealings with the East, extended over a long period, increase whatever perceptive powers a man is capable of, that there are cases when a novice provokes the old resident with confident theories which experience shows to be unsubstantial. This creates an irritation in his mind, and drives him into an antagonism which prevents him on his side from seeing quite truly. Having in one or two cases been justified in his scepticism, he is apt to extend his scepticism beyond all justification. That is only human nature.

The other cause may be that the old resident himself has had one or two bad disappointments. Especially if he brought with him at the outset a somewhat naïve belief that things which go together in Europe, go together universally, that when he heard a certain set of English phrases used he could count on the whole English mentality being there, he would obviously find himself in a number of cases strangely at fault. And then in honest bewilderment at his calculations being thrown out, he would be apt to give up all attempts to understand, to be as clumsily incredulous as he had been clumsily simple. Because the assimilation of Western education has not gone as far as he had first thought, he denies that there has been any assimilation at all. To wiser thought, even the most imperfect forms of assimilation will not be destitute of interest and promise ; it will not " despise the day of small things."

" But even where the assimilation is complete," we are told, " there remains something beneath inaccessible to the European. The ' Oriental ' will be an ' Oriental ' at heart, in the best of cases." Or it is put in the form, " You will never really understand the Oriental." Now, this latter proposition is one which I should not dream of contesting. I quite realize that I shall never understand the Oriental. The only reason why it appears to me hardly worth while making the affirmation is that I shall never perfectly understand any one, not even (perhaps I ought to say " least of all ") myself. Certainly in every other person I know there are thoughts which I never divine, there are regions of mental life into which I can never enter. I am always liable to be surprised by the impulses which spring from that hidden region, to have my expectations thrown out by another's actions. This is so in the case of those nearest to me. Everything which has conspired to make a man different from me— the peculiar nature he inherits from his particular ancestry, the peculiar incidents which have built up his experience

The East and the West

—all this limits my imaginative reproduction of what his inner life is to him. And in the case of myself and a man of another race there are obviously certain factors which will always make us dissimilar. But difference of race is not the only ground of division between men. Where there is no difference of race, other causes of dissimilarity may exist which may create an even greater difficulty in the way of mutual understanding. There are many classes of my countrymen with whom I should find it far more difficult to hold intercourse than with an even moderately educated Indian. The latter and I would have more interests in common.

What is untrue is, not the affirmation that I shall never understand the " Oriental," but the insinuation that because our mutual knowledge of each other is incomplete, it is therefore not real as far as it goes, that because it is imperfect, it is valueless. If I know that my Oriental friend's interest in certain things is as genuine as my own, need it hinder our friendship in this field that there are other regions of our mental life in which we differ ? More than this, it seems to me that where there is on either side the firm assurance of goodwill (and this in many cases happily exists), the diversity of mental constitution is not only no impediment to communication, but gives to communication an added interest, the interest of fresh discovery.

Of course, a great deal is made of instances in which an Oriental, after having apparently become Europeanized, has lapsed on returning to his ancestral environment to the old type, or under the influence of some wave of emotion has thrown off his European culture like a garment. But so far from seeing here anything to disconcert us, I should have thought it wonderful if a large number of such cases had not occurred. No one who knows anything of the inconsistencies and fluctuations of human nature could expect that a new form of culture could advance among any people, with no revulsions, with no inner conflict, with no retrogressions. As if there were no cases in Europe where a man's traditional beliefs subsisted illogically alongside of his acquired intellectual notions! Or as if in England a doctrine once professed always continued to dominate every moment of a man's life thenceforward without a question! But people seem to lose all their common sense and understanding of human nature where the " Oriental " is concerned.

If, however, the view which I have tried to urge is to be judged fairly, it must be guarded against misconceptions on the other side. I may seem to have taken too much for granted that in our rationalism we have something to give the Oriental peoples superior to their native traditions, that Europe has to teach rather than to learn. Now, when I stand back and look as far as I can from the point of view of philosophic history at the result of the last five centuries in Europe, it does seem to me that here a development has taken place in the human family which goes in a certain direction beyond anything reached by man before, a development the fruits of which every branch of the human family must appropriate if it is to go forward in the new time. Whatever they are worth, the qualities associated with rationalism, the power to articulate and co-ordinate experience, to control imagination and belief, have never been brought to so high a pitch before. But I do not hold that rationalism is the whole spiritual nature of man, or that man can live by rationalism alone. It would be no use having the critical faculties which test and co-ordinate experience ever so perfect, if the experience itself were not there. All the primitive body of emotions, all the immediate deliverances of the sense of beauty, the sense of goodness, the religious sense, are things which rationalism does not create, but finds. And failure may come, not through the critical faculties being at fault, but from the experience upon which they play being too narrow. A man, for instance, who has been in love may philosophize upon his passion, but no amount of intellectual sharpness could tell a man what it is to be in love who did not know. So, too, Rudolf Eucken has insisted that while the old Hellenistic philosophy was trying to attain satisfaction by balancing and harmonizing the various elements of experience comprised in the classical world, what Christianity did was to introduce an altogether new experience. To obtain a richer result one may need, not such a strengthening of the faculties as would enable them to get more out of our present data, but an enlargement of the data. Now, every variety of racial character supplies somewhat different material to the critical faculties—one sees the same logical principles work to a sensibly different result in the case of the English or the French or the Germans. And here it seems to me that the extension of Rationalistic Civilization among the Indians or Chinese is likely to bring vast enrichment to the spiritual heritage of mankind. Their new cultures would be rational just as much as the modern European, but they would not be identical with it. Any perceptions of spiritual reality which had gone to creating their ancient literatures, their ancient institutions, would not be discarded, but would form just some of the elements which the rational spirit would reverently assay and formulate and combine in the new synthesis.

The existing civilization of Europe does not present itself as anything final. Its defects are too glaring for us to think that. Only if it is to be transcended it can only be on condition that its lesson is first thoroughly learned. That lesson cannot be passed over or scamped. If the ancient heritage of the Eastern nations in thought and social life is to profit them in the day that is coming, it can only be by its being submitted to the rigid canons of a Reason that has grown strong with all the strength of Western thought. It is a foolish pride that would impel some fervid Nationalists to combat all extraneous influences, to preserve every element of native tradition good and bad alike. Such an attitude may be a natural reaction from the uncritical temper which, having swallowed Spencer and Huxley whole, thought that there was nothing more to be learnt. But it is no less uncritical in its turn. Whatever it may be in economics, *Swadeshi* in the sphere of ideas is a fatal policy for any people. Every spiritual advance which any branch of the human family achieves, it achieves not for itself alone, but for mankind, and any people refusing to benefit by it suffers. After all, there is no faculty possessed by any race of men but is possessed in some measure by all ; the difference is one of proportion. The most primitive savage exercises reason in his own degree ; the rationalism of modern Europe is only the fuller development of something which belongs to man as man. In days when our own ancestors were rude forest-dwellers, the Spirit which

The East and the West

works in human history led men in India and China to new ranges of vision ; again, in the last five centuries the same Spirit has willed the advance of European man to larger powers, and I do not know that any one can demand of Him an account of His election. But what Europe has won, the other peoples, if they are willing to learn, may acquire too. And acquire it they must before they can go on to the next stage. The lesson, if it is not to be scamped, may demand patience in the learner. Two or three generations may not suffice for the learning of it. There is, however, no humiliation in learning, if learning is indeed an increasing mastery of truth. Or if there is humiliation, the people which to-day teaches may have some day to humble itself in its turn to be taught, possibly deeper things than by a rationalistic manipulation of our present experience we could ever discover.

NOTE.

The views combated in this essay were embodied in a book published a few years before his death by the late Mr. Meredith Townsend, entitled " Europe and Asia." His theory purported to have a double basis : (1) in the facts of ancient history, (2) in the facts of modern India. In some articles I wrote at the time I pointed out that Mr. Townsend's assertions in the field of ancient history were wildly at variance with established facts ; in the field of modern India (of which I had no special knowledge) I supposed he might be more at home. On the other hand, I noticed that the reviewer of the book in *The Times* Literary Supplement, who seemed to know modern India, declared Mr. Townsend's assertions in that field to be largely erroneous, though he charitably supposed that his historical reading was " wide and deep." The book is written with remarkable journalisitic facility ; its incorrect statements

Hellenism and Christianity

are thrown out with an easy conversational assurance which would naturally lead an unwary reader to think that Mr. Meredith Townsend knew all about it. One would be unwilling at this date to drag the unhappy book again into notice, if it were not, I fear, still doing mischief. I see that it is referred to as if it were an authority, even by so circumspect a scholar as the Dean of St. Paul's in a recent number of the *Quarterly Review*.

II

BACCHYLIDES

DARK indeed is the night which has swallowed up the great mass of ancient literature and made questionable ghosts of so many immortals. Yet in these latter days it has been broken into here and there by the light of research and compelled in wondrous wise to restore a part, however small, of its prey. Not to speak of unfathered fragments, or of additions to the works which have come down to us under great names, like Euripides and Aristotle, three figures at any rate, which had lost all definiteness of feature, have once more emerged so far into the light of heaven as to become cognizable persons—Herodas of Cos, Bacchylides of Ceos, and, last, Timotheus of Miletus. And it is natural that upon the dead given back a ferment of scholarship should be concentrated which has no necessary proportion to their absolute merits. But little over twenty years have elapsed since a papyrus roll was brought to the British Museum, which proved to contain over a thousand decipherable lines of a poet whom we had hitherto estimated on the strength of a bare 107 ; and already the bibliography of Bacchylides literature in English, French, German and Italian is swollen to an impressive volume. After Dr. Kenyon's *editio princeps* of 1897 three complete

Hellenism and Christianity

editions of the new poems came out abroad, before the poet made, with Sir Richard Jebb's edition in 1905, a fifth, and one might say a full-dress, appearance.

The large reasonableness of Jebb's judgment was signally illustrated by his treatment of the question—which, of course, is one of the first which the name of Bacchylides suggests to the students of ancient literature—whether he and his uncle, Simonides of Ceos, were really pointed at in Pindar's unkind allusions to " vainly chattering crows " and " clamorous daws," the scornful words he flings out from time to time against certain persons unnamed. Jebb was disposed to believe in a real historical basis for the story, told by the Alexandrian scholars, of Pindar's hatred of the two Cean poets. On the other hand, he is well aware how such a story, once afloat, would attract to itself all sporadic expressions of contempt in Pindar, how the learned Alexandrian would discover Bacchylides everywhere ; and he is accordingly sceptical as to the Scholiast's interpretation in the majority of particular passages. The " crow " passage,[1] with its remarkable *dual* verb (γαρύετον), remains as one in which he thinks an allusion to Simonides and Bacchylides probable.

But was there any real justification for calling the " Cean nightingale," as Bacchylides styles himself, a crow ? We are now more able to answer such a question. Bacchylides comes as the final product of a long development, the last of the Nine whom Alexandrian scholarship set apart in the canon, closed for all time, of Lyric Poets. The figure of Bacchylides stands thus as a symbol for one of the great riddles offered by the ancient Greek

[1] " Olymp.," ii, 86.

40

civilization as a whole—the problem why, having begun a new advance along the various lines of human activity, it came in every line within a relatively short period to a stop. Remember that the essential character of Hellenism was that it broke free from the old rule of stereotyped custom in thought and practice, that it brought into operation a new principle, a new standard of reference, reason applied to the real facts of the world. That was the mainspring of its sudden outbreak in great works of literature and philosophy, of art and political construction. And in the principle of reason one might seem to have got a principle of continuous progress. That which existed would always be subject to criticism, go on always being modified, brought nearer to the rational ideal. In our modern civilization, which reincarnates the Hellenic principle, we ordinarily believe that such continuous modification and improvement is going on. But in the ancient Hellenic civilization the promise and potency of its principle in every line of activity, literature, science, art, politics, seemed to meet with an arrest as suddenly as it had begun.

It is a strange feature of Greek literary history that the tradition, instead of remaining fluid and progressive, crystallizes at a certain point fast and immovable. Greek literature is so akin in essence to the European literature of these past centuries, being in a manner its parent, that the contrast it offers in this respect is all the more striking. Sooner or later the line is deliberately drawn; all further development is renounced; the roll of classic masters is closed; there may be imitators innumerable, but fellows of equal prerogative none. Greek literature here seems to correspond rather with Chinese literature than with our own. One would have imagined that if original creative activity continued in any branch of literary composition it would be in lyric poetry, the making of songs. But the arrest in this branch comes quite early in the history of Greek literature, before the great Attic age. People went on all through the remaining centuries of ancient paganism singing the songs of Sappho and other poets of the golden prime, but no new songs were made amongst the Greeks which were thought worthy of remaining in the memory of men.

This is so alien to our thought that we have a difficulty in realizing it, or in understanding how immense the ambition really was, when Roman poets aspired to take rank with the singers of old.

> Quod si me lyricis vatibus inseres,
> Sublimi feriam sidera vertice.

It was indeed the hope of a mortal to break the august circle of Olympus.

Why did original creation stop at this or that point in the ancient world, when in our own world fresh springs of creative invention continue to break out? Perhaps no one will ever be able to answer such a question completely; perhaps an incalculable element will always be there, of which *Dei gratia* is the only account that can be given. Some of the causes may lie back in regions which psychology, physiology and biology have yet to explore. Others, political or social, or related to the special character of Greek literary tradition, we can in a measure make out. Such considerations give, at any rate, peculiar interest to the final stage in the development, to the man who closes the canon. From the historian's

Bacchylides

point of view, as Wilamowitz-Möllendorff somewhere
observes, 250 verses of an inferior poet may be of more
interest than 250 new verses of Pindar or Sophocles.

The political abasement of the Greeks after the Macedonian conquest had, no doubt, much to do with the
cessation of spiritual activity in certain lines, but the
Macedonian conquest did not come till a century after
Bacchylides. During that interval work of the greatest
kind was produced in certain spheres ; but lyric poetry
ran to seed in the new style of dithyramb. Sir Richard
Jebb exposes the futility of the idea that lyric poetry was
killed by competition with the Attic drama. It was the
New Dithyramb, he says, which strangled it. Yet the rise
of the New Dithyramb is less a cause than a manifestation of the process which we want to explain. One may
perhaps ask whether there was not in the Greek literary
tradition itself something which tended to stereotype it
at a certain stage of development.

When we examine the poetical method of Bacchylides
our first impulse is to describe it as a mere " mechanic
art," and to class the Cean nightingale with those many
warblers who have their tune by heart. Its method
looks transparently simple. One seems to start with
some simple statement, narrative or gnomic, as a frame,
and then proceed to bedizen it, as if working with a
Gradus ad Parnassum which supplies a list of conventional
epithets to each substantive, or periphrastic formulas
which may take the place of the substantive itself. To
any warrior you attach an adjective, which means " with
shield of bronze," or " dear to the war god," or " without
fear of battle noise "; to any woman an adjective meaning
" with beautiful robes," or " with deep bosom," or " with

a golden distaff " ; a city is " ancient," or " honoured of
the gods," or " with fine towers," and so on. Instead of
a proper name you may put a patronymic—for instance,
" the son of Amphitryon," or " the son of Perseus,"
or " the son of Zeus undaunted in battle," for Hercules.
Or you may amplify a statement by throwing in a genea-
logical detail of the kind which begins ὃν τέκεν, or some
such formula. These conventions are, of course, part
of the general literary tradition ; but whilst in greater
poets than Bacchylides we look through them—almost
discount them, one might say, in attending to the creative
spirit at work behind them—in Bacchylides they are
given to us as themselves constituting the poetry, as
satisfying our demand by their own merit.

But a merely depreciative estimate of Bacchylides
would leave out of account the conditions under which
he had to work. The object of the poet—to start from
first principles—is to present his ideas in such a way as
not only to convey the logical sense of a proposition,
but to suggest thoughts and images, visual or auditory,
which are the centres of certain emotional vibrations,
vested in an indefinite halo of wonder or charm. Now
it depends upon a variety of conditions what sort of
thoughts and images among any given set of people have
this virtue. Among the Greeks, whose lyric poetry had
come in so large part from ancient religious ritual, invoca-
tions of the gods with many epithets and under many
names, it was, we may believe, the very fact that a phrase
had a traditional ring which gave it the required power.
We may compare the power of Biblical or quasi-Biblical
language over ourselves—a power so signally exploited in
his day by Swinburne. The poetic thrill once associated

Bacchylides

with a definite set of images was apt to become joined
too exclusively to their suggestiveness—the shining of
gold, wind-swift feet, hair coloured like the dark *ion*
flower, voices poignant with honey-sweetness, and the
kindling of desire. To play upon these same strings
over and over again was the way for the poet to make
his effect ; he must speak the emotional language that
the people knew. Pindar, it will perhaps be said, maintained his freedom. But the very effort of his originality,
his continual protest against skill acquired by mere
tradition (the " taught men ") may show that he felt
the tradition stiffening about him. If this be so, the
utterances of Bacchylides in a contrary sense—" Poet is
heir to poet, now as of old ; for in sooth 'tis no light task
to find the gates of *virgin* song "—such utterances have
a peculiar significance. Bacchylides, too, was conscious
of the stiffening of tradition, but Bacchylides had no
heart to struggle or rebel. We may even ask whether
Pindar's somewhat violent originality did not, as a matter
of fact, hinder the appreciation of him amongst the men
of his age ; the Sicilian despot Hiero, καλῶν ἴδρις—if
the statement is true—thought Bacchylides the better
poet.

Greek lyrical poetry, as it goes from Alcman to
Bacchylides, seems to be like a vein of precious metal
which is definitely worked out. The possibilities of new
original invention along that line cease. And one can
hardly help raising the question whether the poetical
activity of our modern European civilization will also
sooner or later work out its different veins. Will a time
come when no one will be able to think of new effects in
poetry, when all poetical composition will be simply

imitation of the models of the past ? Most poets to-day would probably repudiate the suggestion, and yet it remains true that it does become more difficult, as time goes on, to find the gates of virgin song. There are so many simple things which poets could once say with an original note, but which they can say no longer without being commonplace. It becomes harder and harder to combine greatness with naturalness and simplicity. It is easier, of course, to secure originality of a sort by means of the far-fetched and the cranky, but it is a question how much originality of that sort is worth. One notices in this connexion that a modern school of poetry in France believes that the traditional metres of French poetry are instruments out of which nothing further is to be got ; all possible effects that can be produced with the Alexandrine line have been produced ; that vein seems to them worked out, just as much as the lyrical tradition of Greece seemed worked out to Bacchylides.

" Le vers regulier français a, pendant le dix-neuvième siècle, été manié par des maîtres qui semblent en avoir tiré tout le parti possible. Il ne faut pas croire à l'immortalité des types métriques : l'alexandrin ne remonte point à la Genèse et il n'enclôt pas toutes les possibilités de notre haute poésie nationale. Apparu soudain dans la littérature poétique, il a connu un règne long et glorieux. Il n'est point sacrilège de redouter pour lui la caducité qui ne ménage pas des institutions apparemment mieux fondées." [1]

It is a striking contrast between such a view and the view of the Greeks that while the Greeks could conceive of no other possible vein of lyric poetry beside that worked

[1] Paul Duhamel, " Paul Claudel."

Bacchylides

out in Bacchylides, the moderns have high hopes of striking out along new veins when the traditional one is exhausted. That is characteristic of our general optimism as to the future of our modern rationalist culture. We do not think we have come along any line to such a standstill as that to which the ancient culture came so soon after its start. And yet the very mystery of that arrest (for I doubt whether any explanation yet offered for it fully accounts for it) may perhaps give us occasional uneasiness. Might a similar arrest suddenly fall upon our own culture after all its astounding achievements in the last four centuries—a hand laid upon us out of the darkness, some mysterious ineluctable failure of vitality ?

Within his limits Bacchylides is not without his felicities. It was a fine instinct which made him end the " Herakles " and the " Theseus " dithyrambs, one with the bare mention of the poisoned robe, the other with the single line

δίζησθαι δὲ φιλαγλάους ᾿Αθάνας,

awaking the suggestion of glories and of calamities to come, the more thrilling that they were left unspoken and undefined. One can pick out some sonorous phrases which might seem to rival Pindar's, such as

πυργωθέντα πλοῦτον μὴ μελαμφαρέϊ κρύπτειν σκότῳ.

There are similes with picturesque touches which stand out pleasantly, like that of the eagle in Ode V, or of the storm in Ode XII. Perhaps there is no single passage in the new poems quite equal to the familiar fragment

47

Hellenism and Christianity

on Peace, and no single line quite as near to great poetry as the line of Bacchylides preserved by Stobæus—

$$\mu\epsilon\hat{\imath}\zeta\text{ov } \accenthackek{\eta} \; \pi\epsilon\nu\theta\epsilon\hat{\imath}\nu \; \epsilon\phi\acute{a}\nu\eta \; \kappa\alpha\kappa\grave{o}\nu, \; \accentaequistbl{a}\phi\theta\acute{\epsilon}\gamma\kappa\tau\omicron\iota\sigma\iota\nu \; \accentstbl{\iota}\sigma\omicron\nu.$$

It may be that we are justified in gathering from this the reflection, comforting in some degree, that where a part only of the works of greater poets than Bacchylides has come down to us, the selection was not made entirely by blind chance.

III

THE GREEK ANTHOLOGY

THE river of Time, according to Lord Bacon, bears down the lighter trifles and suffers the things of weight and substance to sink. It would be ungrateful to apply the principle to Greek literature as a whole, seeing that what we still possess of it exhibits in the main, although with some grievous lacunæ, its most vital, most permanently important, works. But in regard to some parts of it we must be sensible of a truth in Bacon's dictum. The four thousand or so short poems preserved for us in the collections made by Planudes and Constantinus Cephalas represent a vast poetical literature continuously added to from the great creative days of the fifth century B.C. till far into the centuries of desiccated Byzantine scholarship. In the Anthology poets, whose bulkier epics and more ambitious construc- tions have foundered, still live in a few light lines. In the Anthology we have almost all that survives of the love poetry of the Alexandrine age.

The " epigram " was, of course, originally what the word means—an inscription, words carved on a grave- stone, to give some information as to the person buried below, or on a votive tablet to record the offerer and the occasion. Brevity was dictated by imperious considerations of space and the labour of engraving. By the fifth century B.C. the elegiac metre with its light-winged movement, falling at the end of each couplet to a definite close, had established itself as the normal metre for such memorial verse. The metre was already associated in the popular mind with gnomic poetry, such as that of Theognis and Solon, where also a form apt to hold the memory and well-managed emphasis were first considerations. How soon the inscription took rank alongside of the higher kinds of literary work, how soon it came to be associated with the names of great poets, remains doubtful, since the tradition is doubtful, which ascribes to Archilochus, to Sappho, and to Anacreon some of the epigrams which we possess. With Simonides of Ceos, at any rate (early fifth century B.C.), the inscription, sepulchral and votive, reached supreme literary dignity. However doubtful, even in the case of Simonides, may be the authenticity of much to which his name is set in the Anthology, nevertheless that many epigrams do indeed show us the hand of the great master—the famous Ὦ ξεῖν' ἄγγειλον amongst them—of this we may rest certain.

By the end of the fourth century the short poem in elegiac metre was no longer necessarily intended for inscription. The epigram in the later sense of the word had established itself as a literary *genre*. One class of such poems did not even pretend to be inscriptions. To this class belong most of the productions of the school labelled " Ionian " by Reitzenstein,[1] the school represented by Asclepiades of Samos (end of fourth century B.C.) and his imitators, Hedylus and Posidippus (born

[1] " Epigramm und Skolion," 1893.

about 300 B.C.), literary descendants of the old Ionian elegiac poets. Love and wine are still the theme. And we have only to look at the erotic epigrams which constitute Books V and XII of the Palatine Anthology to see what a long life in Greek literature the type of epigram characteristic of Asclepiades and his school was destined to have. Whether Asclepiades was actually the inventor of the type we cannot be sure ; we must suppose that Plato anticipated him, if we regard the epigrams ascribed to Plato as really his work. It is true that the later erotic epigrams which belong to this line of tradition no longer show the nimble grace, the lightness of touch, the lucidity of phrase, disencumbered of all superfluous ornament and unnatural diction, which marked the epigrams of Asclepiades and his Alexandrine disciples.

Of the other contemporary school, which Reitzenstein calls " Doric," the poetess Anyte of Tegea seems to be the earliest representative in the Anthology. Its great master is Leonidas of Tarentum (first part of third century B.C.). With these poets of the Peloponnesus and of South Italy Eros comes hardly at all into view. In their work another set of motives prominent in later Greek poetry receive literary canonization—the motives inspired by love of the countryside, of woodland and fountain, by interest in the lives of small folk, fishermen, and ploughmen, in the inanimate things which man handles.

> I, Hermes, stand here by the windy orchard
> In the cross-ways near the grey sea-shore,
> Giving rest on their way to wearied men ;
> And the fountain wells forth cold stainless water.

This is a little picture in four lines by Anyte. Like most of the poems of the " Doric " school, and unlike

those of the " Ionian " school, it preserves the form of
an inscription. Perhaps it was really inscribed upon
some stone Hermes, or the form may be only a literary
fiction. In any case it represents the stone as endowed
with conscious life. Reitzenstein suggests that behind
the Tegean poetess lay a long tradition of popular
bucolic poetry, in that Arcadia where the old music lived
on till the days of Polybius. Leonidas of Tarentum
bequeathed to poetical tradition a form of epigram in
which the later poets were never weary of exercising
themselves, the epigram which purports to be the dedica-
tion by some humble worker of the instruments of his
craft—fisherman, huntsman, goatherd, carpenter, husband-
man. The motive gave a fine opportunity to Leonidas,
who, in contrast with the " Ionian " school, loved fine
words drawn from the older literature and charged with
rich epic or lyric associations. To invest by their means
a catalogue of homely utensils with an ideal dignity was
not only a pleasant exercise, but the way to produce an
effect of peculiar piquancy. How far his later imitators
went beyond him in elaboration, how they laid the
swelling epithets thick upon the traditional scheme, may
be seen by comparing his graceful spring song [1] with the
later compositions which make variations upon it. Where
Leonidas says simply " The meadows flower," the
Byzantine scholar has " At her fruitful birthtide the
fair-petalled mead flowereth out of rosy cups." [2]

The influence of Leonidas upon the epigram of later
ages is conspicuous. In later poets, indeed, the various
influences cross and combine. Meleager of Gadara (first
part of first century B.C.), the greatest poetical force in

[1] X, 1.   [2] X, 16.

The Greek Anthology

Greek literature after the bloom of Alexandrine scholarship, whilst, as a writer of love poetry, he derives much from the "Ionian" school of Asclepiades, follows Leonidas in his use of rich ornament. The mass of epigrams after those of Dioscorides (middle of third century B.C.), the last of the Alexandrines, are reproductions of the stock themes in the conventional literary phrases—academic work with more or less grace and felicity. Sometimes, indeed, the living world which surrounded the poet's study broke through his imaginary Arcadia. The passions which were abroad in the days when Rome and Macedon came into conflict find some voice in the verses of Alcæus of Messene (round about 200 B.C.). Still later, at the establishment of the Roman Empire, Philodemus of Gadara (first part of first century B.C.), in his light dissolute verses, and Crinagoras of Mitylene (born about 70 B.C.), household poet of the world-rulers of the day, show touch with real life. In the last age of classical literature, under the Byzantine bureaucracy, we get the strongly personal figure of Palladas (beginning of fifth century A.D.), which, however deficient in the graces and in melody of language, is informed with a rough and fierce sincerity.

We are perhaps apt to think too exclusively of the masterpieces produced by Athens in her great days as constituting Greek literature. It is just its difference from these Attic works, which gives later Greek poetry a particular interest. We are conscious of a change of mood. "There grew up," Dr. Mackail puts it, "a thing new to literature, the romantic spirit. Pastoral poetry, with its passionate sense of beauty in nature, reacted on the sense of beauty in simple human life." "The charm of the country was, perhaps for the first time, realized ; the life of gardens became a passion, and hardly less so the life of the open air on hill and meadow, of the shepherd and hunter, the farmer and fisherman." Perhaps this temper was not quite so new in Greek literature as Dr. Mackail supposes. It may be that if we knew more of the older Greek poetry outside the Attic sphere—of the lost lyric poetry, for instance—we should discover that much which appears to us new in the poetry of the Alexandrine age was really the continuation of a tradition which had been temporarily obscured by the splendid Attic genius. In what remains to us of the older lyrics —of Alcman and Sappho—there are hints of a love of birds and flowers, of an attention to details in nature, which suggest that all through there were more phases in the Greek mind than the concentrated and bridled energy of Attic thought suffered to appear. As has been indicated above, there is a possibility that Arcadia had a tradition of bucolic poetry long before the Alexandrine age. But whether the Alexandrine age brought a new interest into being, or allowed one already existing to come into a new prominence, the significance of the change of mood remains.

The relics of contemporary art are perhaps the best commentary that can be had on the Anthology. Here we see the same interests, the same motives, interpreted to the eye. Graven gems, bas-reliefs in marble (such as those we can study in Schreiber's splendid collection of photogravures), the wall-paintings of Herculaneum and Pompeii, copied as they are largely from the works of Greek masters, furnish illustrations to the text of the poets which should be firmly associated with it in thought.

The Greek Anthology

How — to take a parallel case — could we in England understand anything of the meaning of Japanese poetry, if we did not associate its delicate small pictures with the actual pictures of Japanese art ? And to the ancient Greek bas-reliefs, paintings, and gems we must turn in order to see, as the poets saw them, the country scenes with wayside shrine and herm, the old trees hung with votive offerings, the shepherd and the cowherd, the family group which Death has broken, the Nymphs and Satyrs, the winged Loves in a hundred fantastic combinations. If a selected number of epigrams could be published side by side with good reproductions of the works of art which severally offered a close parallel, we should have no mean help towards a vital apprehension of the long-perished world reflected for us in the Anthology.

The sentimentality, the sensuousness, the love of "nature" and everyday things—all that distinguishes Hellenistic poetry and Hellenistic art from the Olympian poetry and art of the Attic age—bring it in some ways strangely near to modern types of thought and feeling. It is almost startling to the classical scholar to find the modern phrase "charm of nature" ($\phi\acute{v}\sigma\iota o\varsigma$ $\chi\acute{a}\rho\iota\varsigma$) actually used in speaking of the advantage which the country has over the town.[1] Perhaps this very resemblance tempts one, in reading the Anthology, to import into the Greek verses what our mind has really gathered elsewhere, to give a value to words other than that which they had for those who used them. A simple example will make plain what I mean. Meleager prescribes for his own epitaph the words $\Delta\hat{\omega}\rho o\nu$ $"E\rho\omega\varsigma$ $'A\acute{\iota}\delta\eta$, which Dr. Mackail translates, quite legitimately, "Love's gift to Death."

[1] " Anth. Pal.," ix, 360.

Hellenism and Christianity

And yet it cannot be questioned that words like " Love "
and " Death " have become charged for us with a mass
of dimly felt composite associations different from those
contained in " Eros " and " Hades " for a Greek poet of
the last century B.C. Especially when the two words
are joined in a single brief formula, such a formula has
for us an inherent mystical power due to the thousand
times we have known Love and Death coupled with
connotations quite different from the ancient ones in
literature and art from the Middle Ages onwards. To
a Greek of Meleager's day would the phrase have meant
more than that death had been brought on by a physical
passion which wore out the bodily frame? Meleager
has turns of thought and phrase parallel to those of poets
in the fourteenth century. Yet the laughing, wanton
Cupid who fills the veins of the Greco-Syrian with fire
is worlds away from that grave figure whom Dante met
on a day " come peregrino leggermente vestito, e di vili
drappi," or saw in his chamber as a youth clad in raiment
of exceeding whiteness, and whom he called Lord.

If it would be instructive to compare the Greek treatment of Nature with the modern, an even more striking
parallel and contrast is furnished by the poetry of the
Japanese. The results might be extremely interesting, if
any one with a sufficient knowledge of the two languages
would carry out in detail a σύγκρισις of the Japanese
tanka and the Greek epigram. For the analogy of the
two is curious. In both cases among a race of fine artistic
sensibility a form of poetry was developed, the aim of
which was to express a single moment, emotional or visual,
with the greatest possible economy of words and the
maximum of effect. And, so far as one can judge by

The Greek Anthology

translations, such as those of Mr. Aston, the similarity
of idea and expression is in some cases extraordinarily
close.   One fancies that the little poem by Anyte already
quoted would almost conform to the Japanese canon.
Or compare this Japanese poem—

> Fall gently,
> O thou rain of spring !
> And scatter not
> The cherry flowers
> Until I have seen them.

with the Greek (in Dr. Mackail's version)—

Vine that hastenest so to drop thy leaves to earth, fearest thou
then the evening setting of the Pleiad ?   Abide for sweet sleep to
fall on Antileon beneath thee, giving all grace to beauty until
then.

Still closer is the resemblance between the Japanese—

> It is dawn ;
> I cannot sleep for thoughts of her I love.
> What is to be done with this cuckoo
> That goes on singing ?

and the Greek—

All night long I sigh ; and when the grey dawn rises and grants
me grace to sleep for a little, the swallows cry around and about
me and drive me back to tears, thrusting sweet slumber away ;
and my swollen eyes keep vigil, and the thought of Rhodanthe
returns again in my bosom.   O envious chatterers, be still.

The differences, no doubt, if any one followed out the
comparison, would be as striking as the resemblances.
The love of the Greeks for roses and whispering trees
perhaps would seem faint beside the passionate ecstasy
with which the Japanese dwelt upon cherry-flowers and
new-fallen snow.   Sometimes the reticence and allusiveness

of the Japanese would have a subtler power than the frankness and directness of the Greek. The Greek's compass would probably be found larger, if his vision were less penetrating and fine. And where the Japanese abandoned reticence and allusiveness and spoke out his meaning directly, he might seem at a disadvantage.

> Since we are such things
> That if we are born
> We must some day die,
> So long as this life lasts,
> Let us enjoy ourselves.

This seems tame beside—

Often I sang this, and even out of the grave will I cry it : Drink before you put on this raiment of dust.

IV

THE FIRST CONTACT OF CHRISTIANITY AND PAGANISM

THE development during modern times of what is called the "historical imagination," the growth of descriptive psychology and accumulative anthropology, has made the task of the historian seem far more delicate and difficult than it was in former generations. What we now want to do with the documents of the past is something far more ambitious than what our fathers attempted, and yet we must realize, in a way they could not have done, how hard that ambition is to satisfy. The "facts" of history in the narrower sense of the word—the issue of a battle, the promulgation of a law, the establishment of a religion—have a rational interest, we perceive, only in connexion with a larger context of human life, a life which was actually the experience of individuals, and involved a whole world of ideas, of emotions, of desires. What the battle, the law, the religion really were is events in such a life, in such a stream of experience, only as such have they any significance for us. We want to re-live that experience imaginatively ourselves, to feel how it was affected by the events, or the statement of them does not give us anything real. Even where history seems to occupy itself with statistics or naked " facts," which can have no imaginative content, it does so only because these things ultimately bear upon a life which we can more or less realize in imagination, because they serve to explain causes which made it what it was. And it is just this context of past events, this atmosphere of ideas, emotions, and desires, that it is so hard to re-capture. Not only because the millions of individuals in which they existed have, with the exception of some one or two here or there, left no record of themselves at all. More than that, modern psychology has taught us to realize in truer measure the disconcerting variations between individuals in their inner life, and in a still greater degree the variations in the *mentality* (that is the convenient catchword) of different races and different ages. We can never completely understand the person closest to us. And what are we to say of an ambition to understand the buried world of a thousand or two thousand years ago from the scraps of writing, shreds merely of their life and thought, bequeathed us by some score or so of individuals ? We must acknowledge at the outset that our end can never be more than very imperfectly attained. Probably, however intelligently any one had read up modern India or Japan, he would find, on going there, a good deal to correct, a vast deal to supplement, in his impressions. But the accessible literature in England on India or Japan is far more extensive than the literary remains of any period of antiquity. The most finished modern scholar would, no doubt, find much to surprise him if he were dropped into the Athens of Euripides or the Rome of Augustus. And yet our ambition is not utterly vain. We may hope to achieve a measure of success. And

First Contact of Christianity and Paganism

that for the reason that these variations are, after all, variations in a common human nature, differences in the relative proportion of elements, none of which are wholly absent in ourselves. This feat of entering into another mentality than our own we have to achieve in studying both alien peoples of to-day and the men of old time. And in the case of the latter there is the added difficulty which comes from the niggardly amount of our data. We can hold intercourse of question and reply with living Indians or Japanese, but for the past we have to make what we can of the limited number of words set down in writing once for all, whose inexorable silences no questioning of ours can ever fill. How often it is just where we want most to question that the silence comes! And yet even in reference to this there are considerations which encourage. For one personality is not always revealed to another according to the amount of speech. Often a single phrase of our friend has in it a world of revelation. It is not impossible that the broken speech which has come down to us from the men of old may bring kindred spirits into touch across the gulfs of time, may carry a real communication of personal life, quick and powerful, far beyond the dead letter. So to charge words with personality is indeed the magic of great literature.

At any time between eighteen or nineteen hundred years ago some millions of souls were going through the experience of life in the countries ruled by Cæsar round about the Mediterranean Sea. In some cases where the cities of to-day—Rome, Smyrna, Alexandria—are full of eager and various life, a life no less eager and various was being lived on the same soil, in sight of the same hills and seas. In other cases, Ephesus for example, a place which was then covered with streets and market-places, a great hive of men, is now silent marsh and field and barren hill, where the wild grasses grow among what is still left of marble colonnade and theatre. All that life is what lies behind the few volumes of written matter which the age has bequeathed to us ; that life was the context of which they are torn fragments. To some extent the interests which made up that life need no special illumination in order to understand them. They were the same as in any other human society which is concentrated in great cities. Thousands of those genera-tions also were mainly occupied, in the years allotted them, with the hopes and anxieties of industry and traffic, the state of the Roman or Alexandrian market, or the mood of the tumbling sea between Brindisi and Durazzo. Thousands lived for the excitement of loose adventure in the dark archways and the lascivious lanes. For thousands the happiness of life lay just in the daily return from dull mechanic labour to the evening meal with wife and child. There were the periodic festivals when the cities kept holiday, days looked forward to by poor men and slaves, full of the noise of flutes, of glittering proces-sions with the city's idols, lewd buffooneries in the theatre, bloody fights in the arena—the abundant gaieties of the children of the South. There was but little in all this to distinguish the men of nineteen hundred years ago from the populations of Southern Europe to-day.

These things made up a great part of the world into which men of that day found themselves born, a world large and shining and manifold. But for us this particular world round about the Mediterranean nineteen centuries

First Contact of Christianity and Paganism

ago has an interest of an altogether peculiar kind. Something happened in it so momentous, it is believed, that it marks a new beginning in human history. Our popular reckoning, looking back upon the past, divides it into the years before and the years after an event which took place at that moment of time. Into the stream of passing generations there entered just then, there was seen for about thirty years, Someone who has been ever since the great problem. He was not among those who, while they were here, wrote down words which men may still read. He wrote nothing. All we know of what He was, of what He said, is from the memories of His friends. But what was written in those memories was of such a sort that the world has never since been able to escape from the personal force which grasped it through that reflection.

That is why men to-day take up more intently than ever the scraps of writing through which we can get broken glimpses into the past, trying whether a more determined concentration of mind upon the old phrases, a more minute analysis and classification of the contents, a fresh straining of the imagination to read between the lines, may not enlarge, even if ever so little, the opening through which we look into the world where the name "Christians" was first heard. We know, for instance, with fair assurance, that in one of the years of the Emperor Claudius, some nameless person in the harbour town which is now Salonica received a letter, to be read aloud in the little religious association of which he was one of the presidents, beginning, "Paulus and Silvanus and Timotheus to the Assembly of the Thessalonians in God the Father and the Lord Iesus Christus," the first time that the Name appears in the literature of the world. We can read the letter still, but what were the echoes its phrases awoke in the minds of those who first heard it ? What body of ideas did it presuppose as already there, as its background, to use the common metaphor ? The more that little assembly, gathered in the house of some well-to-do citizen or resident trader some morning when Olympus stood blue over against the sunrise, exactly as it does any morning now, becomes realized in our imagination, the more tantalizing does it seem that those bowed heads, those strangely ardent faces, are for ever beyond the reach of our questioning. The Man, whom you call " Lord "—what do you know of Him ? What words, what actions do you connect with the name of Jesus ? What is the image of Him in your hearts that has made all the old objects of your worship seem to you vain idols ? These are Christians with no New Testament ; they are not troubled with any " Synoptic Problem " or " Johannine Question." It does not seem worth while to write down a record of Him whose bodily presence they feel so palpable and urgent. It was only yesterday He was heard and seen and handled ; and to-morrow He will be here again. Is it even worth while doing work of any sort in an interval so brief ? Perhaps some of them will live long enough to have a little book one day put into their hands, whose author will begin by stating his purpose to write down a narrative of those epoch-making events, as he had learned them from those who had seen ; but that cannot be for many years to come. It is hardly likely that any of them will live long enough to see another book, which speaks of the Logos become flesh. We may well believe indeed that when

First Contact of Christianity and Paganism

that book began to circulate, aged saints who unrolled it for the first time at the end of a long life spent in the fellowship of the Church may have asked rather dubiously whence it came, and whether the words written in it were ever actually spoken by "the Lord." If so, their state of mind at that moment in regard to the new book must have resembled curiously that in which some good people find themselves again after eighteen hundred years.

But to go back to our first Christian document, the letter which was read one morning in the reign of Claudius to the brethren at Thessalonica, we find here not only the first mention of Jesus, but a moment in the world-transforming process, most of which is dark to us, or can only be guessed at. Of all the leading men of the Christian community in its first days, there is only one whose personality and course are illuminated for us by writings which are undoubtedly his own. The track of Paul shines curiously in the mists of primitive Christianity, but it was for the most part by persons whose names were soon forgotten in this world—undistinguished evangelists, or itinerant traders, or slaves—that the Good News was carried from city to city, " till the whole was leavened." It is only as one moment or another in the process is revealed to us by some chance notice in a surviving document that we can form any idea of what its progress had been in the intervals—those intervals that were in fact so big with wrestlings and labours, with hopes and disappointments, with agonies and joys. It is in a field beyond our ken that the new thing in the world first meets with the old body of ideas, emotions, and desires which made up the mentality of the Greco-Roman world.

Hellenism and Christianity

That contact, so far as it can be discerned, must be from any historian's point of view a fact of enormous interest. It suggests a variety of questions. What really was the character of the Greco-Roman civilization, what was its mental temper and outlook, as untouched by Christianity? How far did it lead men to repel, how far to welcome the new element? Where it entered into combination with it, how much of either persisted unchanged in the fusion? How far was the fusion a healthy development, how far a corruption of either or both? Probably questions such as these involve considerations too deep for any merely historical argument to reconcile conflicting estimates. It is certain a man might spend his life in a study of the data and feel at the end of it that he could only give tentative answers. No more will be attempted here than some unmethodical reflections on certain aspects of the problem or group of problems.

And, in the first place, one may remark that some difficulty arises from the distribution of our data. Regarding them as windows through which we want to look at a particular action passing outside, they show us separate parts of the field, which it is difficult to combine into a unity. The ordinary classical scholar constructs his picture of the ancient world (or did till recently) from works which were composed for the ruling or literary class. But society, then as now, was distributed in many strata and groups, and it is neither in the *salons* of Rome, nor in the lecture-halls of Athens and Alexandria, that we shall gain much knowledge of the New People. A Roman man of the world like Pliny had only the vaguest notion who the Christians were till he came across them as the governor of an outlying province. In

First Contact of Christianity and Paganism

the middle of the second century the Emperor Marcus still only sees them, from his exalted seat far off, as an unhappy people who have a diseased love of dying in the arena. If any notable man, like Flavius Clemens, Domitian's cousin, was won to the new community, he withdrew from the world's eyes, and the world had little care to acquaint itself exactly with the nature of his " contemptible inertia." We should need to rub shoulders with the crowd on the harbour-quays, to stroll, like Horace, about the fraudulent circus and stand by the fortune-tellers, to listen to the talk of the Syrian merchants at night behind the barred shutters of their shops, to accompany one of the groups of poor Asiatic Greeks who are drawn by some fascination on the Jews' Sabbath to the worship of the synagogue, before we could know the field in which Christianity made its first conquests.

It might not have mattered so much that the literature at our disposal was composed for circles which stood above a certain level of culture or social prestige, whilst Christianity was operating mainly below that level, if that literature had known the " realistic " note which distinguishes the literary ideals of our day. From George Eliot to Mr. Arnold Bennett, it has been the ambition of many writers, whilst writing for the literary class, to render with photographic adherence to fact the life of the unlettered. But the standards of the literary class in the first century A.D. had been strongly conventionalized. The Greeks felt themselves in literature as much tied and bound to the traditions of a creative epoch which lay behind them as we do in the matter of church architecture. Their minds, as they took up the pen, turned away from the vulgar present to the days of

Hellenism and Christianity

Pericles and Demosthenes. The very language they wrote in was in process of becoming artificial, bound to much closer conformity with the old Attic idiom than was the living speech of the day. The enormous place taken by the study of rhetoric in all the education of the time tended further to widen the distance between literature and life. As a window for looking into the past, literature of this kind must suffer from a certain opacity.

And meanwhile we may, of course, without straining to see exactly the point where Christianity and the old civilization come into touch, content ourselves with looking out of various windows one by one. This is very much what Mr. Glover does in his book " The Conflict of Religions in the Early Roman Empire." He does all that humanity (*literæ humaniores* combined with human insight) can do, to read the heart of Virgil, to restore the feelings which led men to hang upon the words of Epictetus, or go repeating the strained phrases of Seneca, or converse with Plutarch in his sleepy, sunny old Bœotian town. And then he will lead us to another window, and we see Justin, the philosopher turned Christian, arguing with a Jewish rabbi in a colonnade at Ephesus; and through another Celsus scanning gloomily the dark barbarian cloud on the northern horizon; and through yet another the decorous Christian *bourgeoisie* which is controlled by the beautiful and earnest, if somewhat rambling and bedazzled, spirit of Clement of Alexandria. As a series of individual studies, a sort of spiritual iconography, of the first century, Mr. Glover's work is a contribution of a very valuable kind to the study of the field. So far as his representation involves

First Contact of Christianity and Paganism

questions of ultimate values, there are, of course, bound to be divergent opinions as to its truth. We shall hear it said on the one side that his estimate of the value of Christianity is excessive. And Mr. Glover might perhaps reply that his book was not intended to be an argument of mathematical cogency, but simply a piece of personal testimony as to what he, looking at the matter as steadily and completely as he can, sees in Christ. On the other hand, Mr. Glover will come at some points into conflict with those who hold the Catholic view as to the origin of the ecclesiastical and sacramental system which is admittedly found to prevail in later generations. And here again we see that neither view can be established as a mathematical proposition, that historical data only yield conclusions of varying probability, and that in the estimate of probabilities, personal feeling and considerations other than historical must necessarily come into play. All we can ask of any one attempting the task which Mr. Glover set himself is that he shall give the data as comprehensive and candid attention as he can, and tell us what impression they make upon him. We should be grateful to any one who does this—especially to any one who does it with so large an apparatus of scholarship as Mr. Glover's—whether we agree with him or not. Ultimately the only way in which such impressions can be checked is by other people studying the same data as a whole by themselves and giving an honest report of what they find.

It would no doubt be a mistake to suppose that the stratum of society in which Christianity first spread was uninfluenced by the ideas and estimates which obtained in circles of a more fastidious classical culture. In all ages the ideas and estimates of the upper class have worked powerfully upon the classes below. We have to think of the people which was first gathered into the Church from among the Gentiles as shaped in large part by those influences. The rhetoric which was cultivated in the schools made—we may see by our authorities— a wide popular appeal. If only a limited number of people, specially instructed, could produce the elegant phrases and cunningly modulated periods, there would seem to have been a large multitude sufficiently educated to appreciate the finished product. Language, as a fine art, provoked much warmer general interest than it does now. Professional orators wandered from city to city side by side with strolling musicians and athletes. The celebrated ones drew crowds, and their coming was as the coming of Paderewski or Duse to a European town in our own day. The more trivial the subject chosen for their theme, the more admirable was the display of their powers. It was no question of original thought or new ideas or natural passion. The demand they had to meet was for phrases only, phrases which should give smooth delight to the ear and play upon that body of subtle reminiscences which constitute the charm of literary diction. Yet in this way the commonplaces of the schools, the old platitudes dressed out as profundities, became an enduring element in the consciousness of the crowd—platitudes which had, after all, at the outset represented a genuine discovery in human experience, and which carried on in a stereotyped form some of the intellectual gains inherited from the greater days of Hellenism.

Even a spirit like St. Paul's was not insensible to the

First Contact of Christianity and Paganism

standards likely to be applied to him by a Greek audience. Charged as he felt himself with something of immense moment, something wonderful and new, to say, he was aware that their attention would rather be directed to observe whether the manner in which he said it corresponded with certain conventional norms. And in regard to that demand he had a consciousness of incapacity which—it is interesting to learn it from himself—almost paralysed him with nervousness. He rose above that weakness by determining to fling all the rules of the fashionable rhetoric to the winds. He would say what he had to say in the directest, simplest way possible, his marvellous story about a Man who had been put to the death of a slave. He would speak, not according to the artifices of the school, but as carried along by the Power that mastered and lifted him.[1] We see now, looking back after so many centuries, that the preachers of the New Life, in breaking through the traditional literary conventions, in disregarding Atticism, prohibition of hiatus, and all the rest, were not sinking to a lower level, even from the literary point of view, but rising to a higher. The things which we seek in great literature —sincerity, originality, life—were just what those conventions stifled. In respect of sincerity, originality, and life, the written or spoken word of the Christian left the learned phrase-making far behind. It is significant that in the sketch of Greek literature which a great Hellenist, Wilamowitz-Möllendorff, contributed not long ago to " Die Kultur der Gegenwart," Paul of Tarsus is given a prominent place. " That this Greek of his has no connexion with any school or with any model, that

[1] I Cor. ii, 1–5.

Hellenism and Christianity

it streams as best it may from the heart in an impetuous torrent, and yet is real Greek, not translated Aramaic (like the sayings of Jesus), makes him a classic of Hellenism. Now at last, at last, one can hear in Greek the utterance of an inner experience, fresh and living." It is only judging by very false and artificial standards that Paul can appear, as Bossuet represented him, a speaker destitute of power and charm, effective purely by a transcendent miracle. Simply as eloquence or literature, 1 Corinthians xiii is superior to anything in Dio Chrysostom.

It is unfair to say that all those who mediated between the schools and the crowd sought simply to enchant by goodly phrases. The figure of Epictetus would rise up to confute such a statement. The audience indeed which gathered round Epictetus seems to have been drawn from the upper classes, but in his own person Epictetus linked them to the class of Asiatic slaves from which he came. As a slave, he had first found his stay in the severe formulas of the Stoics ; and he was not the only one of his class, we may be sure, to whom those formulas brought strength and self-respect. If we were to consider those elements in the environment of early Christianity which belonged to the classical tradition of Greek civilization, to the tradition cultivated in literary circles and in the schools, the tradition which the old-fashiond scholar was apt to take as completely representative of the first-century world, Stoicism would unquestionably be the element of prime importance for the Christian Church. For in Stoicism the mind of antiquity had not only reached in some respects its highest expression, but that expression had become popular in a way unparalleled in the history of any other school. The

First Contact of Christianity and Paganism

Stoic missionary, preaching the self-sufficiency of virtue in a threadbare cloak at the street-corners, had been one of the typical figures of a Greek town for many generations before St. Paul. But, after all, the classical tradition only supplied some of the elements in that world. For our present purpose we will rather turn our attention to certain other influences shaping its mentality, influences much more powerful probably than any of the strictly classical elements among the classes of lower social standing—petty traders, freedmen, slaves—which in the first instance offered a field to Christianity.

Scholars, it would seem, are beginning to hold that Greek literature all through, beginning with Homer, had tended to be governed by a certain artistic instinct of elimination in its picture of life. All the time, it is thought, there was a substratum of primitive superstition, of unsatisfied religious cravings breaking out in wild or grotesque ways, which it was not " the thing " to touch on more than very slightly in literature. It is probable, for instance, that there were various animal or semi-animal deities worshipped among the Greeks at the time the Homeric poems were composed, but Homer knows nothing of any gods save human ones. Primitive rites, again, intended to propitiate the ghosts dwelling in old graves, Homer, according to this view, knew of and ignored. And the same instinct continued to work in greater or less measure throughout the successive phases of Hellenism. In our day, of course, when the study of anthropology and comparative religion has come in with a flood, it is just the traces of every savage survival and the cults reaching out fervently into the unknown, upon which avid researchers fling themselves. By catching at every hint dropped by our authorities, and piecing them out by analogies and imagination, we can to some extent get behind their reticences. And sometimes the earth is kind enough to yield a broken tablet with the formulas of a forgotten sect. Probably the dominance of ideas of this order was actually smaller during the two centuries of intense political life which were the classical age of Greek literature. Interest ran too strongly in other channels, and active minds found the daylight preferable to mysteries. But the traditions of primitive magic, the Dionysiac and Orphic and Pythagorean confraternities, continued to find their votaries, and then when the city-state and its official religion, under the shadow of the Macedonian and Roman world-powers, ceased to satisfy the needs of the individual, all the rites over which hung some veil of mystery exerted a new attraction in a world ill at ease.

But by that time other influences had begun to come in ; elements of the older civilizations of the East had begun to penetrate the Hellenic world in a volume impossible before the conquests of Alexander. In magic, it is the strange and unfamiliar which is imposing, and now the Greek townsman was given his choice of numberless varieties of magic with all the prestige of barbaric names and unintelligible formulas. Worships of Isis and Osiris and Serapis spread from city to city. Chaldean astronomers came into universal request. Between the occult religions already rife in Greek soil, the Orphics and others, and the new influences from the East there was a natural affinity. Anthropology has revealed a great family resemblance between the myths and super-

First Contact of Christianity and Paganism

stitions of primitive people all the world over, and the stories told in New Zealand or among the Zulus to explain the genesis of the world are not much more childish than the cosmologies of the old Babylonians, or Egyptians, or Indians. In India, in Egypt, in Greece, as civilization matured, men found occult meanings for the bits of primitive practice which had come to look uncouth to them, and the naïve stories of their fathers they turned into philosophical allegories. The conceptions of the Greek occult sects and many of the ideas contributed by Babylon and Egypt were akin, partly because at the back of both lay the same fund of primitive superstition, partly because both represented the essential tendencies of the human spirit struggling from primitive super-stition to something dimly understood. The propagators of these beliefs regarded them as the sacred deposit of some god or god-sent sage in a remote divine past ; they were wisdom, profound because very ancient, like the " secret doctrine " still believed in by dabblers in the occult. To-day most of us would say that the old times were in fact the childish times, and the revelation lay rather in the goal which an inner impulse was driving men on to find.

As a result of all this mixture—Greek philosophical dogmas, Orphic and Pythagorean beliefs, ideas from Egypt, ideas from Babylonia, ideas from Persia, ideas from Judæa, with a plentiful dose of crude old magic —we seem to get a floating, ill-def.ned body of popular belief, which Reitzenstein has named " Hellenistic theology." It lay, before the modern zeal for anthropology and comparative religion, outside the purview of the ordinary scholar. One of its principal documents,

Hellenism and Christianity

the little collection of writings under the name of Hermes Trismegistus, still waits for a critical edition, though Reitzenstein has prepared the way in his interesting book "Poimandres." It is, indeed (except for some stout-hearted member of the Theosophical Society who boggles not at the wildest products of the human imagination) a rather joyless study. And yet of all the constituents in the atmosphere breathed by the infant Church, this is the one which will probably present Christian theologians in the near future with their most delicate problem. We may say, indeed, that the study of all that mass of things denoted by Reitzenstein's "Hellenistic theology" on modern lines has only just begun, although the standards of scientific research have been set up in the field by a number of illustrious scholars, Usener, Dieterich, Reitzenstein, Bousset, Cumont, and others. The material by which that dim world can now be disclosed to us is no doubt scanty. And we should have even less than we have at present, had it not been for the large infiltration of elements from "Hellenistic theology" into the Christian Church, with the result that they came to exercise the pens of its leaders, largely in a polemical sense. For even the view that supposes the most extensive absorption of Hellenistic elements by primitive Christianity admits that at a certain point the line was drawn. The Church after a struggle expelled from its body a kind of doctrine which its leaders pronounced to be an alien poison. This was the Gnostic Crisis of the second century. The Gnostic teachers, as we see them now, were not a set of men who gratuitously, or for the mere pleasure of indulging their fancy, or from a morbid rage for speculation, spun a web of arbitrary

First Contact of Christianity and Paganism

nonsense. They simply drew from the current tradition of the heathen world. It was inevitable that many persons steeped in that world of ideas and coming under the influence of the Gospel should try to combine the two things. Behind this Christian or semi-Christian Gnosticism presented to us in patristic literature there lay a great volume of purely pagan Gnosticism, whose documents have almost entirely perished. But the Christian Gnosticism, studied in connexion with such things as the Hermetic writings and what we know of the old Babylonian, Egyptian and Persian religions, helps us to understand the character of that obscure background.

The Gnostics (this point has been well put by Anz) were not primarily moved by a speculative interest, but by an essentially practical one. We must try to throw ourselves into the feeling as to life which seems to have prevailed among the great masses of the people in the Greco-Roman world. When men looked up to the stars, they shuddered to see there the Powers whose mysterious influence held them in the mechanism of an iron necessity. These were the World-rulers (κοσμοκράτορες) who fixed men's destiny without any regard to human will and human tears. Effort, shrewdness, long-laid design could bring no liberation from the predestined law. And especially it was the Seven who bore rule, the five Wandering Stars with the Sun and Moon. Long ago watchers had marked their courses from the towers of Ur and Erech, and now when the old Babylonian religion was come to its dying phase in the lowland of the Euphrates, the astrological element in it had grown at the expense of all the rest. It was from Babylon that this fear of the stars, and especially of the Seven, had spread through the Roman Empire. It became an obsession. This earth, the sphere of their tyranny, took on a sinister and dreadful aspect ; even after death the disembodied ghost would be hemmed in by the demons of the air ; the unknown spaces above, the Unknown on the other side of death, were full of terrors. But Hellenistic theology could point out a path of deliverance—for some men at any rate. Sphere rose above sphere, shutting men in, but beyond all, far, far away, the Great Father abode in a realm of bliss, above fate and death and evil gods. And the wonderful thing was that in men (*some* men, the Gnostics said), in men creeping on the low earth, in bondage under the Elements, there was something, a spark, a seed, a breath, which belonged by origin to that far-off divine world. Platonism came in here to fill out the conception, Platonism with its doctrine of a world of real Being beside the base world of matter and change, a world of pure, eternal Reason, to which the soul in virtue of the reason in it could win its way. This made men feel that the evil of the earth consisted in its material substance, and that the divine element in man was just his mind ($νοῦς$). But how was a man to escape from the prison-house, to get through all those enveloping spheres that rose, one above the other, the realm of the Seven, and regain the natural home of his spirit beyond them all ? How else than by mastering the celestial topography, by knowing the order of the gates he would have to pass, by knowing what God or demon would confront him at each gate, and the proper password for each ? It was all-important, for instance, that when his soul was confronted by the god with the lion's head,

First Contact of Christianity and Paganism

he should be able to say instantly, " I know thee for Jaldabaoth," or whatever the name might be ; for it was an old idea that to *know* a demon, to name his name to him, was to deprive him of his power to thwart. All this *knowing* was *gnōsis*. The interminable lists of uncouth barbaric names which Irenæus tells us the Gnostic had to learn by heart had thus as practical a bearing as the names of streets in Chicago would have for me, if I expected to be stranded there, dreary as a list of them might appear to be here and now.

With this general idea at the basis of them all, the countless sects showed considerable varieties in the way they elaborated it. In some—in those in whom the Greek strain predominated—the speculative interest did, no doubt, come to take a large place. Their interest was to some extent directed to the questions, " What is the world, and how has it come to be ? " apart from the individual concern for salvation. And then we get the picture of the Upper World (the *plerōma*) filled in with a plurality of divine beings, we get schemes of successive emanations, more and more complicated, or beside the Father the figure of the Mother becomes prominent. Bousset has given ground for thinking that in the Mother we have the old Semitic Ishtar (Astarte), who had been at once in strange fashion the virgin-goddess and the goddess of lust and prostitution. Her double character in tradition explains how in the different forms of Gnosticism the Female Power is sometimes associated with the Father, sometimes with the malignant Seven, and sometimes is a Power who belonged originally to the Upper World, but has fallen to the lower region. To the Syrians an amalgamation of such conceptions

79

with Christian belief was rendered easier by the fact that the word for " spirit " is feminine in the Semitic languages. The Mother and the Holy Spirit coalesced, even in such a case as that of the anti-Christian Mandaïte sect (still lingering on in a small way about the Euphrates region), amongst whom the dark aspect of the Mother prevailed, with the strange result that the " Holy Spirit " is here an Evil Power. There were again various ways of explaining how this anomalous condition of things—an evil world beside the good one, imprisoning an element which did not belong to it—came to be. Sometimes the fall of a Divine Power was itself the explanation, sometimes the evil world had been created by the lower Powers, by an inferior Demiurge, or by the Seven themselves, and then various explanations had to be found as to how the element from the Upper World had come into it. With some sects greater stress was laid on ritual and practice, various sorts of baptisms and markings and sacraments ; these were held necessary in order to liberate the divine element from its material entanglement. Some insisted upon abstinence from flesh or from wine. Most attention was, of course, drawn to a force whose working is as wide as humanity, and which has in itself an ever-fresh potency for provoking curiosity —the sexual impulse. It could not fail to preoccupy the thoughts of the Gnostics in a special way. It seemed to be the very force by which the World-ruler secured the continuance of his kingdom, and those who were set to break his bonds must frustrate him here, if anywhere. Some sects took the high ascetic line ; the impulse was to be altogether suppressed. With some the end seemed to be gained in obscene sacraments which gave vent to the impulse and yet disappointed the World-ruler of his desire to see new generations born under his yoke. Asceticism and lubricity are often plants springing from the same soil.

All this to a modern man may appear intolerably unreal and fantastic. The daylight levels of ordinary classical literature, the cheerful philosophy of a Horace, even the tragic mood that is induced by the palpable evils of the world—pain and injustice and separation—these things have meaning for him, but he will perhaps feel grateful that the feverish nightmares of antiquity have left as scanty record as they have. For him the skies, as far as the utmost star, are clear of any malignant Intelligences, and even the untoward accidents of life are due to causes comfortably impersonal. We have never been thoroughly frightened ; the ancient world was frightened ; there is the great difference. The possibility that the Unknown contains Powers deliberately hostile to him is one the ordinary modern man can hardly entertain even in imagination—though why, if it contains conscious beings of any sort, these should necessarily be friendly rather than hostile it would perhaps be difficult to prove from the fragment of the Universe accessible to our senses. And till the Unknown has been realized as something terrible, till we have had the feeling of help-lessness and ignorance in the face of an immense Universe, the feeling of a lost child in a huge strange city, we can hardly understand the mood which led men so eagerly to seek for " knowledge " and catch at anything which seemed to promise them light and safety. Speaking generally, indeed, of the ancient world about the Christian era, it has often appeared to me—I do not know whether

Hellenism and Christianity

others have got the same impression from the documents
—that the fear of death was much more powerful and
more widely diffused than it is among ourselves. When
the Gnostics spoke of the world as " evil," they seem,
for one thing, to have had prominently in mind the
subjection of men to death. A New Testament writing
speaks of men as being " through the fear of death all
their lifetime subject to bondage." [1] The phrase is
striking ; one could hardly use it with regard to our
contemporaries. We probably know a number of people
who stand apart from the Christian hope, and yet do not
seem to be in bondage to any continuous fear. If we
suppose this element in the mentality of the ancient
world, various things acquire new meaning. The philosophic writers labour, for instance, with what seems to
us unnecessary persistence to fortify men against this
fear. Possibly what makes us find a writer like Seneca
theatrical and wearisome is that in this respect he no
longer " speaks to our condition." Perhaps the finest
part of the poem of Lucretius is his passionate argument
why men should not fear death—but would a modern
materialistic poet have thought it necessary ? To such
a mood the announcement of the resurrection of Jesus
must have brought a thrill difficult for us to realize—
the supreme Dread not only met, but actually defeated
within the world men knew ! We can understand too
why the side of the new teaching which soon became
pre-eminent amongst the Greeks was its promise of
immortality ($\dot{a}\phi\theta a\rho\sigma\acute{\iota}a$).

But it is not only the historical impulse, the desire to
enter imaginatively into the life of a bygone age, which

[1] Heb. ii, 15.

First Contact of Christianity and Paganism

may induce us to give our attention even to something so repellent as the Gnostic phantasmagoria. For the questions which such a study raises touch us at a vital point—those of us, at any rate, who hold by the Christian hope. For Christianity has always involved a number of assertions as to the supersensible world ; Christianity has claimed to give an interpretation of the significance of Jesus in relation, not only to human history, but to the transcendent Reality behind the world. A Christian cannot therefore brush aside assertions relating to that region, simply because they venture beyond the limits of sensible observation, with the same immediate decision as an Agnostic. He is in the more delicate position of having to show the assertions of the Gnostic to be fantastic without compromising the soundness of his own. More than this, Christianity and Gnosticism are not only alike in overleaping the bounds of sensible experience ; they both came into the world in the same age, under the same intellectual and spiritual conditions. If, then, Gnosticism is to be rejected as an unprofitable play of the imagination, the question naturally suggests itself, What part belongs to imagination in traditional Christianity ? Nor is the putting of this question merely an abstract possibility. Christians are confronted to-day with a formidable body of opinion which actually maintains that a great part of Christian belief was formed of notions current in the Hellenistic world, and has no greater validity than the Gnostic conception of the Mother and of the Pleroma. This is the view to which Continental Protestantism has in large part rallied ; Harnack has explained in detail how Christian belief, as it appears by the end of the second century, represents

Hellenism and Christianity

a "Hellenization" of the original Gospel, the process having begun already in the New Testament.

The fact cannot be denied that when the early preachers of Christianity explained the position of Jesus in the totality of things, they did so in terms which bore a close resemblance to conceptions already current in the heathen and Jewish worlds. The problems which arise out of this fact will perhaps be the most crucial ones for Christian theology in years to come. To throw Christianity and Gnosticism alike overboard, as creations of unregulated fancy, is, of course, one way of dealing with it—the way of writers like Salomon Reinach, a rough-and-ready way, which soon leaves us face to face with all the philosophical difficulties involved in a view of human life exclusive of the transcendent. There is the way of Liberal Protestantism, which excises everything transcendent except belief in God the Father and in the survival of the human soul. But it seems to be increasingly evident how difficult it is to maintain these two beliefs in isolation from what has been their living context, since trench they undoubtedly do upon the transcendent sphere. Nor does the idea of maintaining Christianity as a system of emotional morals appear to have much promise—if by morals we mean something which excludes an outlook beyond this present world —since of such morals we can find purer exponents than Him who came to bring a sword upon the earth and trouble men with far-stretched hopes and gratuitous agonies. The pain for which Jesus is directly responsible in the world can only be justified if man is really in his eternal being what Christians believe ; it is useless pretending that the transcendent in the character and teaching of

First Contact of Christianity and Paganism

Jesus is something easily detachable, without which the rest holds good all the same. But if we maintain the transcendent beliefs of Christianity, what are we to make of the Hellenistic parallels ? It does not, of course, follow that, because an idea formed part of the current mental stock of the age before the advent of Christianity, it had no validity ; theologians may urge the universal working of the Divine Spirit and the principle of inspired selection. I should not wish to deny that such answers point in the right direction. At the same time it may be that the difficulty of some of the problems has not yet been fully faced. The plain man, it is true, need not be troubled by finding that an idea he has acquired from the teaching of the Church or of his Bible had already been made public by earlier teachers, if the idea is independently verifiable in experience. If, however, he believes it solely on the authority of Church or Bible, as a divine announcement, there would perhaps be some reason in his disquiet at discovering that the idea could have been familiar by the most ordinary human channels to those whom he supposed to have spoken directly from God. Or, again, granting that both within the Christian Church and outside one Divine Light shone with varying radiance, the task of deciding what is actually the eternal element and what the ephemeral, of distinguishing the Real from the Symbolic, the essential idea from the outworn vesture, is one for which the Christian Church may need in the time to come the most strenuous exercise of its thought, the closest experimental converse with spiritual realities.

We have dwelt on the fact that Christianity assimilated elements from its Hellenistic environment. But there is also the other side. An inspiration for selection implies

Hellenism and Christianity

an inspiration for rejection. And it is obvious that Christianity was something with a very positive life of its own, which rejected vigorously much that it came in contact with. It would be absurd to imagine that the Hellenistic theology as a whole which, under the guise of Christian Gnosticism, tried to establish itself within the Church, was compatible with the principles of the Christian life. At many points the antagonism was profound, and it is perhaps the less necessary to insist upon this as the contrasts have been forcibly put by the writers on Church History. Dr. Charles Bigg's chapter on " Gnosticism " in his posthumous " Origins of Christianity " is taken up entirely with insisting on the contrasts. To his fine and true spiritual frame the elements of baser superstition in Gnosticism were particularly repulsive, and, it may be, they deserve the contemptuous abhorrence with which he handles them. Yet it is certainly something of a disappointment, when he raises the question, " How far did Gnosticism affect the Church ? " to find that he means only " How far did the Gnosticism which was ultimately rejected by the Church obtain a temporary footing ? " It is, of course, plain that Gnosticism, definitely marked as such, had a very limited vogue in apocryphal gospels and pious romances. Only two elements does Dr. Bigg point to in passing as having struck root in the Church—asceticism and the worship of the Virgin. It is interesting to note that the Anglican writer is in a position to stamp these elements of Roman Catholic Christianity as alien accretions with no more compunction than Harnack shows in doing the same thing for various parts of the theology which Anglican and Roman have in common.

First Contact of Christianity and Paganism

Even at first sight the Gospel must have presented in some ways a striking contrast to " Hellenistic theology." It must have seemed such a simplification. Instead of the enormous apparatus of mystical words and ceremonial practices, to believe that in order to conquer all possible terrors of the Unknown, the whole range of ghostly enemies, one needed only to know Jesus ! It must have been like the lifting off of a burden to say " I believe in One God, Maker of heaven and earth." Christ had left His community indissolubly attached to its spiritual progenitors of the old Israel. There was something in the Hebraic element, the specially Synoptic element, in Christianity—so far all may find a truth in Harnack's view—which saved it from being carried away by the Hellenistic current. The Christian could never look with the Gnostic's abhorrence upon the earth and all the conditions of bodily life ; to pray continually " Thy will be done on earth as it is in heaven "—that alone set him on the side of the Hebrew prophets and at variance with a theology for which the earth was incurably bad, and escape from it the whole of salvation.

Perhaps few books seem less ethereal than Ecclesiasticus in its sober-going morality, its pattern of ordered family life, the strong, earth-treading family tradition of the Hebrews. And it may seem surprising that a Christian mystic like Clement of Alexandria should draw his quotations from this very book with notable frequency. We may see, however, that while the Gnostic was wishing to fly forthwith above the stars, it was just a tradition of domestic pieties which kept the Christian (who also regarded himself as a stranger and pilgrim in this world) content to discharge meantime the business of life and

Hellenism and Christianity

submit himself to laws which were not the Devil's, but God's. The distance which the Christian Church swung in the direction of asceticism after a few generations shows how strong the pull of contemporary forces was ; but there was always something which held it back from the Gnostic ascetic extreme, no less than from the opposite Gnostic extreme of lawless indulgence. The Christian, like the Gnostic, might feel that there were spheres of hostile or obstructive power surrounding him. Indeed, many of the phrases of St. Paul, " the Prince of the Power of the Air," " the World-rulers of this darkness," " angels and principalities and powers," have obvious affinity with contemporary pagan and Jewish Gnosticism. And St. Paul seems to have conceived of these Powers as opposing themselves to intercourse between God and man. But all that opposition—here was the difference —all barriers, all distance were annihilated by the love which, reaching down from the highest, held the redeemed man in an immediate grasp. " I am persuaded that neither death, nor life, nor angels, nor principalities, nor things present, nor things to come, nor Height, nor Depth, nor any other creature, shall be able to separate us from the love of God, which is in Christ Jesus our Lord."

V

THE GNOSTIC REDEEMER

W E may, I suppose, say that the questions raised by the study of Gnosticism and the things akin to it in the ancient world are those which at the present day probe most searchingly into the fabric of Christian belief. Probably many theologians even to-day hardly realize the weight of the difficulties which are bearing upon them from that quarter. Gnosticism is a field into which they have never thrown more than perfunctory glances. And there is a good deal to deter any one from doing more than this. For the field is not an exhilarating one. To wander among the febrile fancies and unwholesome imaginings which sprang up in such rank abundance at a certain period of human history is undoubtedly depressing for a healthy-minded man.

It is a remarkable testimony to the neglect in which all that class of things was left till recently that for the principal document of non-Christian Gnosticism, the little collection of writings which go under the name of " Hermes Trismegistus," there exists no tolerable modern edition. In the sixteenth century, when there were still scholars who believed that it enshrined a sublime truth, the little book was had in honour ; when the belief in its religious authority faded, it was thrown aside,

Hellenism and Christianity

and the old text printed in 1574 has never been improved upon.

And now this deserted field finds itself once more the centre of new interest, though interest of a very different kind. The movement which is covered by the words Anthropology, Comparative Religion, combined perhaps with that branch of Psychology which concerns itself with religious phenomena, has created an eagerness to lay hold of all that is most eccentric, obscure, and subterranean in belief and practice. These students have none of the naïve faith of the Theosophist in a secret revelation underlying the superstitions which they treat ; it is rather that they find in them psychological laws or historical connexions which set the higher and more reputable religions in a new light. It is not that they wish to raise crude superstitions to the level of the higher religions, but rather that they wish to show large elements in the higher religions to be of the nature of crude superstition. It is for this reason that the new study of all those strata of ancient religion which lay below the daylight world of the old classical scholar—of magic and Orphism, of mystery cults and Gnosticism—forces questions upon the Christian theologian with which he is bound to grapple. Christian Gnosticism, it is now recognized on all hands, was not a wanton perversion, a wanton sophistication, of a clearly articulated orthodox theology, but an attempt made by men, who had received the Church's teaching when its intellectual expression was still more or less wavering and tentative, to combine that teaching with conceptions and aspirations prevalent in the Gentile world whence they had come. And we have to reckon to-day with the assertion that attempts of this sort did

The Gnostic Redeemer

not begin with Simon Magus, or whoever was the first Christian Gnostic. It is asserted by the dominant school of *Religionsgeschichte* that already in the Apostolic Age the infiltration of pagan belief and practice into the original Gospel had begun.

Beside the sacramental system, Christology is the department where the influence of pagan conceptions is most often alleged. It is asserted that already in those passages of the New Testament which speak of a Divine Being who for our sakes, though He was rich, became poor, of One who, being in the form of God, took upon Him the form of a servant, of One who, being the express image of God and upholding all things by the word of His power, made cleansing for sins and became a little lower than the angels through the suffering of death, of the Logos, the only-begotten God, who became flesh —it is asserted that here we have the apostolic generation drawing upon the same body of pagan belief as that upon which the Gnostics drew later, when they constructed their Syzygies and Æons.

A great deal in Gnosticism presents close resemblances to what is found outside the circle of Christianity and Judaism. In so far the Gnostic schools are special forms of a type of belief and practice which had become largely diffused throughout the Hellenistic world about the time of the Christian era. It is this type of belief and practice which has been illuminated in recent years by such workers as Dieterich, Reitzenstein, Usener, Cumont, Bousset, and others. Reitzenstein terms the floating body of beliefs " Hellenistic theology." It is one of the products of the mixture of Hellenic and Oriental traditions which took place after the conquests of Alex-

Hellenism and Christianity

ander. Some elements seem to have an Egyptian origin, others a Babylonian, others a Persian ; there are obvious affinities with the belief and practice of the older mystic sects of the Greek world, Orphic and Pythagorean ; and everywhere one traces the effect of the great Greek philosophic schools, the influence of the thought of Plato, the influence of the Stoics. Some form or other of this " Hellenistic theology " had probably become the *Weltanschauung* of most of those who had any living religion in the world of Greek culture—cruder and more superstitious forms of it in the lower strata of society, more refined and Hellenized forms among the educated, the Syrian-Greek Stoic Posidonius being perhaps the cardinal personality who prepared the Western world to receive much Oriental tradition in a Greek guise. All forms of this " Hellenistic theology " had apparently certain common ideas. There was first the fundamental conviction that the world accessible to the senses, this material world, was evil—or at any rate very inferior to the transcendent world of light. There was next the conviction that in the soul of man somehow or other an element from that Divine world had got mixed up in the material sphere. And lastly, there was the conviction that by some means or other the Divine element could free itself and win its way back to the sphere whence it came. Of course endless variations were possible upon this common theme. The evil of the world might be described under various aspects. There might be various theories of the constitution of the superior world, all sorts of complications in transcendental topography. Various explanations might be given as to how this abnormal state of things had come about—a Divine

The Gnostic Redeemer

element imprisoned in a world to which it did not belong. There might be all sorts of ways of redemption—magical formulas, baptisms, sacraments, abstinences, interior exercises, intellectual illumination.

The ancient Hellenist does not seem to have thought of the evil of the world quite as the modern pessimist is apt to do. Probably any one nowadays talking of the evil of the world would be thinking primarily of the injustice of the actual state of things, the imparity of the distribution of good things with desert, the pains of poverty and disease and oppression. In Hellenistic theology this aspect of things is not prominent. By the evil of the world they seem to have thought firstly of the transitoriness of material things. They wanted to reach something abiding and unchangeable. The contrast of γένεσις, Becoming, with that which is ἀγένητον and eternal—this runs through all their language. How far this is due to the influence of Plato, and how far the Platonic tradition is itself only one expression of a wider feeling in the ancient world, is a question which might be discussed by those whose knowledge in this field is fuller than mine. Secondly, the evil of the world seems specially connected with sensual passion ; there is the persistent contrast of πάθος, and especially ἐπιθυμία, with that which is ἀπαθές and ἀπροσδέες, without passion and without needs. It is as well to realize clearly that the New Paganism which has sounded its note in modern literature, the cry to abandon the " pale Galilean " for something more full-blooded, more flushed with sensual enjoyment, in so far as it glorifies ungoverned impulse and vehement passion, is curiously unlike the real temper of the old pagan world. Even in the great days of Attic literature, ungoverned impulse and vehement passion were things looked upon with dread and disgust, and as the ancient world grew older it seems to have felt more poignantly the weariness and burden of its lusts. Probably the glorification of these things in the modern world is just an indication that in the modern world they have grown tamer. We can afford to pat the beautiful tiger upon the head, which to the ancient world was too fierce and terrible a destroyer, too enormous in its ravages, to appear as other than the chief embodiment of evil. Thirdly, the evil of the world seems to have been connected about the time of the Christian era with the domination of the stars. Men were " in bondage under the elements of the world." The astrological beliefs which from Babylonia had penetrated Hellenistic society had represented the lives of men as determined by an iron necessity from without, by εἱμαρμένη, the influences of the heavenly bodies. It was not every one who had the confidence of the Stoic that if his life was governed by a resistless Law, that Law was at any rate a Divine Reason to which he could joyfully assent. To large masses of men the world, this earth at any rate, was governed by powers either indifferent to their good or actively malignant. Such a conception made the world appear a prison-house from which the human soul cried to be delivered. And the Hellenistic theology averred that the prison-house had limits, that there was a sphere above the realm of the stars, if only the soul could find its way thither. And surely it might, if there was something in the soul itself which had come thence and belonged to that sphere by natural right.

This general view of the world is common to such non-Christian thought as is represented by the mystical

The Gnostic Redeemer

Hermetic writings, possibly in part pre-Christian, and to the Gnosticism which claimed to be Christian. But in this Gnosticism the scheme of things includes a prominent figure, a *Sotēr* : there is not only a way of redemption ; there is a Redeemer. Now in so far as this Redeemer is identified with the Man who taught by the Lake of Galilee, there is no question whether we have a Christian or pagan doctrine ; but the question may be raised whether primitive Christianity and Gnosticism fitted to Jesus of Nazareth the conception of a Redeemer older than Christianity, a conception which existed originally apart from Him, or whether it was the Christian belief in Jesus which induced the Gnostics to introduce the figure of a Redeemer into a scheme which had originally been framed without one.

It may seem that an attempt to prove that the Christian Christ was new would be a vain attempt to prove a negative. For it is merely some few scraps which we have of the beliefs of that various Hellenistic world, and who can say what conceptions may not have been cherished among sects and conventicles of whom all record has perished ? I think we must admit that we cannot prove anything in this field in the fashion of a mathematical proposition. Nor do I think that Jesus would disappear if some anticipation of Catholic Christology were discovered in a pre-Christian papyrus. Yet when it is asserted that, as a matter of fact, the Christian belief in the Redeemer was an element taken over from current Hellenistic theology, I think we may rightly ask for proof of it.

There are, of course, considerable variations between the doctrines of one sect and those of another as to the

Hellenism and Christianity

person of the Redeemer. They agree that in Jesus a pre-existent heavenly Being was present upon earth, but as to the manner of his corporeal manifestation they show a variety of speculations. All alike, I think, regard Jesus Christ as a compound, even more so than the Catholic Church, whose doctrine of two distinct Natures coexisting in one Person presents the modern theologian with terms which rather seem to require an explanation than to afford one. With the Gnostics the human nature of Jesus is either a mere illusion, the Docetic view, or so detached from the Divine that we have really two persons. Where the latter view is held, the man Jesus is regarded as having been originally distinct from the heavenly Christ. Because he was the wisest and purest and most righteous of men, the heavenly Christ descending entered into him—at his baptism in the ordinary theory —and the compound Jesus Christ came to be. In the " Pistis Sophia " the coalescence of the two is put at an earlier moment in the life of Jesus. His mother Mary narrates : " When thou wast small, before the Spirit had come upon thee, whilst thou wast with Joseph in a vineyard, the Spirit descended from on high and came to me into the house, having thy likeness, and I had not known him, but thought that it was thou." Mary goes on to relate how the Spirit asked, " Where is Jesus my Brother ? " and how she tied the stranger to the bed while she went to seek her son. When Jesus is brought, the exact resemblance of the two figures is seen. The Stranger is set free ; whereupon " he embraced thee and kissed thee, and thou didst kiss him, and ye became one." [1] According to Carpocrates, Jesus was

[1] " Pistis Sophia," 61, p. 78.

The Gnostic Redeemer

the son of Joseph and Mary, a man distinguished from other men only by his greater strength of mind and will, in virtue of which a special spirit of power had been sent down into him from the Father.[1]

On the other, the Docetic, hypothesis, the man Jesus did not really exist at all, but was only a shadow, an illusive appearance,[2] the sole reality being the heavenly Christ. And between these two views there seem to have been other theories of the compound Jesus Christ which gave him an earthly nature of a kind, though not a really human one. His body was real, but did not consist of ordinary matter : it was, according to a Valentinian teaching, " a body framed by an occult art, to have the accidents of matter, visibility, palpability, impressibility, but not real materiality." [3]

All these theories had the great point in common that they separated the idea of suffering from a Divine Being —an association of ideas peculiarly repugnant to the Hellenistic mind. On the Docetic hypothesis the Passion of Jesus was an appearance only, like all the rest of his visible life : on the other theory the suffering was real, but it was only the man Jesus, and not the heavenly Christ, who was the sufferer. For as the two had once existed in separation, so they were again separated before the death upon the Cross. For instance, in the system of the heretic Justinus, the heavenly Being, here curiously called Baruch, leaves the body of Jesus upon the cross ; and crying out to Edem, that is, to material Nature, " Woman, behold thy Son " (Γύναι, ἀπέχεις σου τὸν υἱόν),

---

[1] Irenæus, i, 25, 1.
[2] ἐν σχήματι καὶ ἰδέᾳ μόνῃ, Epiphanius, 23, 1.
[3] Irenæus, i, 6, 1.

97   G

Hellenism and Christianity

reascends to the Supreme.[1] A trace of the same idea is found in the Gospel of Peter, where the cry upon the cross is given as, " My strength, my strength, why hast thou left Me ? " In Clement's Excerpts from Theodotus, the theory is modified by saying that the Spirit who descended upon Jesus did not separate from him at the Passion, but contracted himself, so that death might take effect (οὐκ ἰδίᾳ γενομένου ἀλλὰ συσταλέντος, ἵνα καὶ ἐνεργήσῃ ὁ θάνατος). Otherwise death would have prevailed over the Sotēr, which is absurd, ὅπερ ἄτοπον.[2] A peculiar theory of Valentinus seems to have been that the sufferer was not Jesus, but Simon of Cyrene, crucified in his place by a divinely ordered confusion.

It is important in this connexion to notice that the idea of Jesus Christ being a composite Being does not stop simply with the separation of the Jesus from the Christus. There seems to have been a desire to find in him a bringing together of all the elements of the Universe, as it were the Pauline idea, ἀνακεφαλαιώσασθαι τὰ πάντα ἐν τῷ χριστῷ, turned inside out. The Heavenly Person is indeed in some schools simple, either the Father Himself, as in the sect of Simon, or an emanation from the Father ; but occasionally we find him represented as the product of a plurality of heavenly Powers, Æons,[3] or even of the whole body of Æons, the Pleroma, κοινὸς τοῦ πληρώματος καρπός,[4] or in another phrase πλήρης τῶν πληρῶν.[5] When we come to the lower elements in Jesus Christ, we find more than simple manhood. Where, as

[1] Hippolytus, 5, 4, § 26.
[2] Exc., 61.
[3] Epiphanius, 35, 1.
[4] Hippolytus, 6, 2, § 32.
[5] Hippolytus, 5, 2, § 16.

98

The Gnostic Redeemer

among the Ophite sect of Hippolytus, there is a triple division of the Universe into νοερά, ψυχικά, and χοϊκά, Nous, Soul, and Earthy Matter, all three are found combined in Jesus Christ, and the text πᾶν τὸ πλήρωμα εὐδόκησε κατοικῆσαι ἐν αὐτῷ σωματικῶς is applied to this fact. It comes to very much the same thing where the body of Jesus is explained to have been not of ordinary matter but itself, in whole or part, psychic or spiritual.[1] And here we get an interesting connexion between the constitution of Jesus and the descent of the heavenly Christ. The Gnostics, in agreement with Hellenistic theology generally, thought of the earth as being separated from the upper world of light by a series of intermediate spheres. There are usually seven of these, as the conception is taken over, as a matter of fact, from the Babylonian star-lore, which attached especial importance to the sun, the moon, and the five planets, and thought that each of these heavenly bodies was fixed upon a sphere of its own, whilst the spheres revolved, one outside the other, around the earth. It was these seven which determined by their influences all that happened within them : of this shut-in *kosmos* they were the *kosmokratores*. Their influences had come, as we have seen, to be felt as a crushing iron necessity, and here upon earth was the divine imprisoned spark, which belonged by right to the transcendent world beyond all the Seven Spheres, to the Eighth Region, the Ogdoad. The Seven Spheres thus appeared as barriers between the soul and its true home : there were gates indeed in the barriers, but they were guarded by the demonic lord of the sphere,

[1] Hippolytus, 6, 2, § 35.

who did not easily allow any to pass. Through all these spheres, the Divine Being, who descended from the world of light to deliver the imprisoned element of Divinity, was bound to make his way; and the problem how he passed exercised the Gnostic's imagination. And one common theory was apparently that he passed by a deception; it was by assimilating himself to the kosmo-kratores, by taking on their likeness, that he concealed from them who he was.[1] Connected, perhaps, with this idea was the doctrine that the body in which he taber-nacled was actually composed of elements which he had taken from each sphere in his descent.[2]

The heavenly Christ had not descended in order to die (that, for such a one, was impossible), but in order to reascend, and in his reascent to open the way for the imprisoned divinity in men. He had once more to pass the gates of the spheres. And where it was believed that in descending he had taken elements from the several spheres to form his body, it was taught that in reascending he had laid each of those elements aside in its proper sphere, where four elements take the place of seven spheres.[3] The world-rulers who would bar his passage were overpowered or stricken with terror, and the way was open for the redeemed.

Now, what strikes one in this Gnostic account of the descent and reascension of the Redeemer is that it is just *a reduplication of the Hellenistic story of the soul.* Already, wherever the divine spark burned in the souls of men, a heavenly thing had come down somehow

[1] Irenæus, i, 23, 3; Epiphanius, 21, 2, etc.
[2] Apelles, Tertullian, 6.
[3] Hippolytus, 7, 10.

through those intervening spheres into this place of darkness: redemption consisted in its return. But in those fragments which we have of Hellenistic theology, unmodified by the influence of Christian faith in a human Person, there is no Redeemer; he is absent from the doctrine of Posidonius; he is absent from the Hermetic writings. And why is he needed? For the possession of knowledge is enough to enable the soul to regain its heavenly home, whether by knowledge be understood intellectual enlightenment in the higher Platonic sense, or knowledge of magical formulas and mystic practices in the baser superstitious acceptance. Among the Christian Gnostics again we find elaborate systems of magical lore: by learning the names of the demonic creatures who would oppose the soul on its upward way, the pass-words which were appropriate to each gate, the soul could have power over all its adversaries. But this magical apparatus seems something sufficient in itself, if it really works, without a Redeemer. Salvation by such *gnōsis* and salvation by Christ present the appearance of two alternative schemes which have been imperfectly joined together.

But the parallel between the descent and return of the Christ and the descent and return of the soul is still closer in its details. For just as the Christ formed his body of elements taken from each sphere and gave those elements back at his reascension, so the soul, according to a doctrine which was current about the Christian era, took from the different spheres at its descent that sum of passions which constituted its bodily temperament, and discharged them again on its upward way.[1] Again, just

---

[1] Corpus Hermeticum, i, 24 f.; Servius, ad Æn., vi, 714.

as the Redeemer passed the gates by concealing himself from the world-rulers, so we get the idea sometimes stated that the soul escapes them by being hidden. For instance, in the teaching of some of the Valentinians [1] a chrism of oil and water together with certain occult formulas rendered the soul invisible to the world-rulers : so, too, according to a Cainite sect, the higher Wisdom, in drawing to the upper world the souls which belong to her, hid them from the Maker of this world.[2] In the Acts of Thomas, although the original Gnosticism has been revised in a Catholic sense, we still find this idea unchanged. St. Thomas in his last prayer offers the petition : " May the spiritual powers not perceive me and the world-rulers not conspire against me and the toll-keepers not oppress me ; may the lower and the higher beings not withstand me, but flee and hide themselves because Thy victorious power surroundeth me ! " [3] Here the idea that the soul eludes the eyes of the gate-keepers is combined with the alternative idea that they are intimidated and paralysed by a superior power. Both ideas are found in descriptions of the descent and return of the Redeemer.

What functions can the Christ have in such a scheme ? Well, in the first place, he may be the bringer of that *gnōsis* which enables the soul to rise. In so far he is less to be described as a Redeemer or Sotēr, than as an Enlightener and Revealer. Among the pagan mystery sects, just as universally among the Christian-Gnostics, the occult tradition was regarded as having been delivered

[1] Irenæus, i, 21, 5 ; Epiphanius, i, 36, 2.
[2] Epiphanius, 38, 1.
[3] " Acts of Thomas," p. 91, Bonnet.

The Gnostic Redeemer

originally by Divine inspiration, not seldom by a god himself—by Orpheus, for instance, or by the Egyptian Thoth, who, in the Hellenistic amalgam represented by the Hermetic collection, appears reduplicated as Hermes and as Tat. The author of the first document in that collection, supposed by Reitzenstein to have been the founder of a special sect, describes himself as having been taught by the Supreme Mind Himself in personal form as Poimandres. " Having thus spoken unto me, Poimandres returned to the company of the Powers. And I, having given thanks and blessing to the Father of all things, was dismissed by Him, empowered and taught the nature of the universe and the transcendent vision. And I began to preach to men the goodliness of piety and knowledge (*gnōsis*), saying, ' O people, men born of the ground, that have given yourselves over to drunkenness and sleep and to ignorance of God, be sober, cease from your heaviness, held as ye are in the spell of sleep without reason.' And they, when they heard me, came to me of one accord. And I spake, saying : ' Wherefore, O men born of the ground, have ye given yourselves over to death, when ye have the power to inherit immortality ? Repent, ye that have gone in the way of error and had part in ignorance. Be quit of that light which is darkness, leave corruption behind you and inherit immortality.' And some of them mocked and departed, having given themselves over to the way of death, but some besought me to teach them, throwing themselves at my feet. And I caused them to stand up and became the guide of the race, teaching them the words (which I had heard) how and in what manner they might be saved." Compare with this the Gnostic hymn given by Hippolytus : after describing the human race wandering in the maze, it goes on :—

And Jesus said : " Behold, O Father,
The striving with evil things upon earth,
How it wandereth wide from Thy spirit,
And seeketh to flee from the bitter Chaos,
And knoweth not how it may pass through.
For which things' sake, send Me, O Father ;
I will descend bringing the seals [i.e. the secret words of power],
I will make My way through all the Æons,
I will open all mysteries,
I will reveal the forms of the gods ;
And the hidden things concerning the holy way,
Calling it *gnōsis*, will I deliver."[1]

So far as Jesus appears in the Gnostic systems as the revealer of *gnōsis*, we may admit that he stands in the same category with the Divine or inspired revealers to whom the mystic sects generally ascribed the origin of their traditions. In this function, however, he is merely Prophet, not Redeemer : the important thing is the message, not the Person of the messenger. With the Church it was Jesus Himself who was important. And in the Gnostic sects, the Christ has generally other work to do. And this work we may sum up by saying that it is to do actually what the Divine element ought of its own nature to do, but does not do, in its fallen imprisoned state, through want of power. The Light in man ought to triumph over the world-rulers of this darkness : the heavenly Christ does triumph. The Light ought to rise to its true home in the world of light : the Christ does rise, overcoming all obstructions. His history is, as we saw, the old story of the soul reduplicated : only, whereas the old story of the soul was an ideal which had to be

[1] 5, 1, § 10.

The Gnostic Redeemer

realized, the history of the Christ is an accomplishment. One might almost say that the work of redemption is to bring power to the fallen Divine element in man by a process of sympathetic magic. The Christ does something, and behold the fallen Divinity in the soul is enabled to do it too. "From his appearance," it is said in the Valentinian doctrine as stated by Irenæus, the fallen Divinity, personified as Achamoth, "received power" (δύναμιν λαβοῦσαν ἐκ τῆς ἐπιφανείας αὐτοῦ). In the "Pistis Sophia" power resides in the stream of light which bursts into the dark world, and in that light the strength of the fallen Divinity is renewed.[1] Just as the rôle of Christ had been the ideal of the soul realized, so now the soul becomes assimilated to Christ in his achievement. The assimilation is represented in certain sects as identification. The man joined with the Logos becomes Logos Himself, γίνεται μετὰ τοῦ Λόγου λόγος.[2] "I am Christ," another says, "since I have come down from above through the names of the 365 archons."[3]

In connection with this close parallel between the Sotēr and the soul, we can understand the ambiguity which attaches to such a parable as that contained in the celebrated "Hymn of the Soul." It is ordinarily taken, and I think rightly taken, as the story of the soul; Preuschen and Liechtenhan, on the other hand, maintain that it is the story of the Redeemer. A good case can be made out for either theory, if certain details are pressed. It is that very ambiguity which, for our purposes, is instructive.

[1] Ch. lxv, 77.
[2] Hippolytus, 5, 3, § 21.
[3] Epiphanius, 26, 9.

Hellenism and Christianity

These facts seem, I think, to point to the figure of the personal Redeemer not being an original part of the Hellenistic theology. We can understand that men brought up in the conceptions of that theology and coming upon a set of people for whom the fulness of God dwelt in one human Person bodily, whose whole hope for life, and everything that came after, hung upon Him, might try to find a place for such a supreme Person in their systems, and might find it as the Gnostics did. And while so much in their theories can be shown to have been taken over from current paganism, no real parallel in current paganism has been discovered to the belief, which they shared with the primitive Church, of the Divine One taking upon Him for the love of men the form of a servant, coming into the sphere of darkness in order to redeem. We cannot, of course, prove a negative, but it is noteworthy that there is no Redeemer, as was pointed out, in the Hermetic literature or the system of Posidonius. We have, of course, the conception of Divine Beings who, long ago, delivered to men the arts of life or occult wisdom ; we have inspired prophets and revealers ; we have myths of gods who had been slain and entered into immortality ; we have myths of gods who fought with the monsters of darkness and overcame them. The just craving of the anthropologist to establish connexions must, however, it appears to me, have risen to a degree which destroys the finer instinct of discrimination before he can suppose that by making any combination of elements taken from these one could create the Christian idea of the Saviour. For if Divine self-sacrifice is the very point and meaning of the story as a whole, we do not prove much, even if we succeed in showing that

The Gnostic Redeemer

details of the story are found separately elsewhere. The nearest pagan parallels to the Christian idea seem to me to be found, not in the current Hellenistic doctrines, but in the old myth of Prometheus and in the Indian idea that Krishna becomes reincarnate in each successive age to save the failing cause of righteousness. The myth of Prometheus was, however, at the Christian era a bit of traditional mythology, which does not seem to have held any dominating position in popular thought ; and no serious historian, so far as I know, has supposed that an Indian doctrine is likely to have reached or influenced the first generation of Jesus' disciples. Nor need one insist upon the glaring differences between the conception of the Divine self-sacrifice in the old polytheistic setting and the conception based upon the Hebrew faith in the One God. But it it was the clinging of the Christian community to Jesus which caused the Sotēr to hold a prominent place in the Gnostic version of current Hellenistic theology, and not a previous belief in a Divine Saviour which caused the first generation of disciples to invest Jesus with that character, then one can hardly agree with Pfleiderer's view of the hymns of gratitude and praise to Jesus poured out in the apocryphal Acts of John and Thomas. " The religious interest," he says, " in popular Gnosticism concentrated itself wholly upon the one figure of the God and Saviour Christ, whose exaltation above all powers, whether above the heavens, in the heavens, on the earth, or below the earth, is emphasized in the strongest possible fashion. With the historic Jesus of Nazareth He has indeed little in common but the name. . . . He is for the Gnostic nothing else

than the ' Saviour-God ' of the mystery-cults."[1]   Pfleiderer
does not specify what Saviour-God of the mystery-cults
there was of whom it might be said that " though He
was rich, yet for our sakes He became poor." That the
way the Gnostic worked out his conception of the
Saviour involved a large borrowing from Hellenistic
theology, the facts referred to in this paper, I think,
are enough to show ; but for the central point of devotion
to One who embodied a supreme act of Divine love
and voluntary humiliation there is, I believe, no Hellenistic parallel. May one not rather use the words of
Preuschen ? " This does not signify, as might at first
appear, that the Christian has lapsed into the pagan ;
it signifies rather that the victory of Christianity over
paganism has begun."[2]

[1] " Primitive Christianity," iii, pp. 186, 187.
[2] Since the above essay was written a book by Wilhelm Bousset
has been published (in 1913), " Kyrios Christos," in which all the
analogies which extensive erudition in this field can discover between
primitive Christianity and the pagan cults in its environment are
arrayed together in order to explain the Christian worship of " the
Lord " Jesus.   In such a book it is interesting to find the admission :
" The distinctive Christus-mysticism of the Apostle [Paul], his
' in Christ,' ' in the Lord,' is something which offers a sharply
marked contrast to the ideal of deification prevalent in Hellenistic
piety, even if it shows an affinity with it on certain sides.   The way
in which Paul feels Christ as the over-arching and encompassing
element of his higher spiritual self and at the same time as the
power which determines and sustains the life of the Christian
community—this is something for which any parallel in the religions
of the surrounding world can hardly be found, even if the spiritual-
izing mysticism of the Hermetic writings, for instance, shows some
faint analogies to it " . . . (pp. 172, 173).

VI

BETWEEN TWO WORLDS

AN eminent scholar and man of letters once wrote a book on Ancient Greek Literature, and in its concluding paragraph glanced at the final destiny of the ancient culture and at that which took its place. " The search for Truth," he wrote, " was finally made hopeless when the world, mistrusting Reason, weary of argument and wonder, flung itself passionately under the spell of a system of authoritative Revelation, which claimed a censorship over all Truth, and stamped free questioning as sin."

These words seem to give expression in an admirably concise and telling way to a sentiment very general among classical scholars. In passing from the products of the human mind in the old pagan environment to the products of the human mind under the influence of Christ, they have a sense of coming to something markedly inferior. It is not only a question of some conventional literary standard which has set up a particular phase in the evolution of a language as classical, and regards everything written in other forms of the language as essentially debased. We have all smiled, of course, at the professor who warned his pupils against reading the New Testament in the original for fear of spoiling their Greek; but it is not only scholastic preju- dice. It is not a mere whim which has made one form of Greek and Latin classical; the fashion is based upon an estimate of a greater inherent value in some respect belonging to the literary products of the classical age. Can it be denied that in passing from classical to patristic literature the ordinary humanist must perforce feel that the mind of these writers is working within restricted limits; that their outlook is narrowed by ecclesiastical conventions which have no universal interest for man- kind; that their acuteness and originality have play only within a field bounded by premises which are never themselves examined by free thought? We imagine Plato and Aristotle, if they had been confronted with their Christian descendants, brushing away a mass of ecclesiastical cobwebs with an unsparing hand and recalling thought to the broad basal facts of reality.

If we are concerned to maintain that with Christianity something new of unique value entered the world, we must face fairly the aspect of deterioration which the Christian world offers to the classical humanist. And I suppose we may allow that deterioration as a fact and yet not believe that it was *due* to Christianity. There was a complex of causes bringing about the intellectual decline of the ancient world at the moment when Christ- ianity entered the field; and if it is the Divine plan that the good of mankind should be worked out only in a process of ages, there is nothing to forbid a man's holding that a new principle of life came into the world with Christianity, and that nevertheless its operation was not designed to be so rapid as to prevent the downfall of that particular society into which it was first introduced.

Between Two Worlds

As a matter of fact it has been pointed out—by Dr. Bigg, I think—that if the Christian writers are compared, not with Plato and Aristotle, but with the non-Christian writers of their own time, they show no inferiority on the intellectual side. Origen is not on a lower level than Porphyry, nor Basil than Libanius. Everywhere in the agony of ancient civilization, beaten upon and penetrated by the barbarian mass around it, it seemed the supreme task to maintain as far as possible the tradition of the past—to be stationary seemed an achievement, when the forces making for retrogression were so strong —" having done all, to stand." The authority of the past became the watchword in all departments of spiritual and intellectual activity—in the dry scholasticism of the later Roman Empire, no less than in the tradition of the Church. We may believe that Christianity had enriched life with a new experience, and yet recognize that the minds at work upon the matter of life had not the same elasticity and liberty of movement as the minds which in the fourth century B.C. had been brought to play upon the experience, poorer in this particular, of the ancient Athenian. No theological prejudice need therefore induce us to minimize, no anti-theological prejudice to magnify, the relative truth of the words with which the scholar we quoted concluded his survey of ancient Greek literature.

And yet, as we transport ourselves in imagination back into those times when the ecclesiastical tradition is forming which is destined to confine the human spirit for so many centuries to come, we may feel a desire to force upon these minds, before the shell hardens, some of those ultimate questions which their ancestors had

Hellenism and Christianity

begun to consider. Is there no one at once sensible of the new thing inshrined in the life of the Christian society and able to look at things with the freedom of the ancient philosophy ? It is all very well to see the operation of Christianity upon minds willing to take a mass of traditional doctrine for granted, but how much more interesting if we could discover some mind really quickened with the ancient scepticism and see it confronted with this new thing !

And here we meet the figure of the African professor of rhetoric, Aurelius Augustinus, the figure which embodies for us more than any other the transition from that classical world about to pass away to the world of Christendom. He is the child of the past, awakened to spiritual aspirations by Cicero, steeped to his finger ends in Virgil, one upon whom the rich heritage of the old pagan philosophy has come and whom it stimulates to original thought. And then this same man becomes the Christian doctor who, according to Harnack, more than any other one man shaped the theology and ruled the ecclesiastical practice of Western Europe in the Middle Ages. Nay more—for here too, as in the case of some other great typical figures at crucial points of the world's history, elements are transmitted which remain for the immediately succeeding ages undeveloped germs and only unfold their significance under the conditions of a later day— Augustine's influence counted for much in giving its initial impulse to the Reformation, and yet further, through the revelation of personality, the introspective psychological analysis embodied in his " Confessions," Augustine may appear, as some one has called him, the " first modern man." Here surely is some one with

Between Two Worlds

whom at this moment of transition it would be interesting to converse.

And most interesting, we may add, at the moment of transition in his own individual history—while his outlook has not yet been hemmed in by such doctrines as that the act of two individuals some 4,780 years before is sufficient ground for assigning the whole of mankind to eternal torment—doctrines which have ceased to have much actuality for us—while he can still feel the power and charm of that culture upon which he is going to turn his back, while he is still occupied with the great basal questions—What is Truth, and how can man find it ? Wherein does man's good lie ?—the old questions which had come down to him from ages of unsatisfied search, the questions that are living issues with men to-day—if at this moment of his history we might have speech with Aurelius Augustinus !

And we may—in the most pleasant surroundings. We are at Casciago, on the slopes which go from the uplands called Campo dei Fiori to the Lago di Varese. In our daily walks we have a view to the north-east of the full magnificence of the Pennine Alps dominated by Monte Rosa. It is August, and in the summer evenings the white peaks change to a wonderful rose. The spectacle seems hardly to arrest the attention of Augustine, and his eye passes without interest over the eternal snows. But we may remember that he is a man of the ancient world after all, and that our modern admiration for mountain heights is something quite alien to him. On the other hand, he is quite alive to the charm of the green meadows round about us, still fresh even in the late summer. " *In monte incaseato* " (the mountain of good things of the dairy), "*monte tuo, monte uberi*," he quotes, playing on the name of the place—a quaint text of the Old Latin Psalter, not justified by anything in the Hebrew.[1]

The estate at Casciago,[2] upon which we are staying, belongs to one Verecundus, a worthy citizen of Milan, whose profession of *grammaticus*, professor of literature, in the great city of North Italy, one supposes to have been lucrative. His wife is a Christian, and also, strangely enough, it is she who is the great obstacle to his becoming one himself. For he would be a poor sort of Christian, according to the perverted standards of the time, if after conversion he failed to break off the marital relation. Verecundus wished to be a Christian in the full degree, if he were one at all, and he could not face the sacrifice —"*Nec christianum esse alio modo se velle dicebat, quam illo quo non poterat.*"[3]

Neither Verecundus nor his wife has come to enjoy the refreshment of a *villeggiatura* this August of the year 386 A.D. at Casciago. Verecundus has put the house at the disposition of his friend Augustine, and here accordingly we meet him and the group of persons who have come up from Milan to keep him company. For Augustine has been for two years teaching rhetoric in Milan and is much sought after by young men. He has recently passed through that inner crisis which he will some years hence describe in his " Confessions " as his definite decision for the Christian life. It has been thought that when he looked back upon the

[1] Psalm lxviii, 15.
[2] In Latin, Cassiciacum.
[3] " Confessions," ix, 3.

experience from a later date his memory presented the change as a more abrupt and radical breach with the past than in fact it was. The letters he wrote soon after the event seem to show him still only half a Christian. If, however, we have to allow something for the transfiguration of past experience in memory, we have on the other hand to allow something for the opaqueness of a conventional literary style, which might not allow at first a new experience to show through in all its fullness. If the " Confessions " possibly exaggerate the rapidity of the change, it may well be that the letters reveal it imperfectly, and that the truth is somewhere between the two.

We must see who the others of the group are, gathered round Augustine at Casciago. There is first Alypius, an old pupil of Augustine's long ago in the African township of Tagaste, from which they both came—a small, vigorous man rather younger than Augustine. His parents belonged to the upper circle of society in Tagaste (*primates municipales*). For Augustine since those early days he seems to have had a dog-like affection. He followed him from Tagaste to Carthage. Then the old friendship was knit up again in Rome. When Augustine came to Rome in 383 he found Alypius already there, following his career in the Roman courts. Thenceforward they have been continually together, and when Augustine removed the following year to Milan, Alypius went too. One of those people almost naturally ascetic, we may gather; in the days when he and Augustine were Manichæans together, Alypius contrasted with his friend in making the celibate life, recommended by that religion, a reality. On the legal bench Alypius showed an incorruptibility above the common standard of the time. Next winter, if we are still observing him, we shall see him walking with bare feet over the frozen soil of North Italy. Not that this man, so rigidly self-schooled, has been without his temptations. It was he who was taken to a gladiatorial show against his will and determined to keep his eyes shut, but could not resist opening them at the sound of a great shout ; then caught the infection of the horrible madness, and only escaped from it later on, and with pain. He has been affected too with the vanity of literary purism, and till lately had been unable to spoil the beautiful Latin of his correspondence with Augustine by inserting the barbarian name " Iesus Christus." But in these latter days the two friends have been going through a common experience, and the barbarian name has begun to exercise a strange power upon Alypius.

Then the group includes two young men who have been studying rhetoric under Augustine at Milan, and to whom the retirement to Casciago is of the nature of a reading-party—Licentius and Trygetius. Licentius is the son of a man whom Augustine has known from childhood, and whose help has counted for something in his life. That man is Romanianus, himself too of Tagaste (he is a cousin indeed of Alypius), one of those reckoned very rich according to the measure of those days and honoured with statues and tablets in his native place. The great questions of religion and philosophy have come within his field of vision, but the vast extent of his worldly business leaves him little time and thought to spare. His son Licentius is of an ardent temperament, which will one day run into evil courses, but now fires him mainly with literary ambitions. "*Accepisti a Deo ingenium spiritualiter aureum, et ministras inde libidinibus,*" his old master will write to him at a later date. Now it is especially as a poet he wants to shine, though he is capable of feeling sometimes the superior attractiveness of philosophy. Augustine even writes to his father at this happy moment that to this divine mistress "*totus a juvenilibus illecebris voluptatibusque conversus est.*" His fellow-pupil Trygetius, of Tagaste, like the rest of the party, has come back to rhetoric and philosophy, after a spell of service with the eagles, but finds history, if the truth be told, with its trumpets and clash of arms, more congenial than abstract thought or literary elegancies—"*tanquam veteranus adamavit historiam,*"—"he loved history like an old soldier."

There is also here at Casciago Augustine's bro'her, Navigius, whom we never get to know well enough to pronounce what he has in him, and two who come and go quietly in the background—Lastidianus and Rusticus, Augustine's cousins—saying little, for indeed, though Augustine respects their native common sense, they have hardly had the education to intervene in a philosophical discussion—they have not even passed through the hands of the *grammaticus*; "*Nullum vel grammaticum passi sunt.*" [1] There are lastly two figures to complete the group, each with its own peculiar pathos—the figure of the mother, Monica, and the figure of the boy of fifteen, Augustine's illegitimate son, Adeodatus, in whom so much hope centres and who is destined so soon to pass from this sphere of things.[2]

---

[1] "De Beata Vita," 6.
[2] Ibid. 10.

Hellenism and Christianity

The days in this delightful environment pass pleasantly. On a specially cloudless morning the party will leave their beds early and engage in some sort of country pursuits.[1] But for a good part of most days Augustine's two pupils, Licentius and Trygetius, are working hard at their books under his direction.[2] They are going through Virgil with him—half a book every day before supper is the usual measure[3]—and this part of their studies threatens to inflame the poetical ambitions of Licentius to a degree which the master finds excessive.[4] For him the interest of their intercourse belongs rather to those hours when the little company turns to discuss the large problems of life and its meaning, which in his new phase have come to override all literary and worldly enthusiasms. These discussions take place at no fixed time, as the mood and the circumstances of the day suggest. Sometimes days go past without talk of this sort.[5] Sometimes they do not begin till the sun is already low and the country pursuits and Virgil have had their turn. Sometimes on a fine day they will wander out into the open country and give the morning to philosophy among the green fields. And it seems as if the talk of this little group of men in the summer days of 386 on this Italian upland, significant of a great change taking place in the world, is really to sound on audibly through all succeeding centuries. A shorthand-writer, a *notarius*, has been provided to take record, and

[1] " Adv. Academicos," ii, 10 ; " *in rebus rusticis ordinandis* "; ibid. i, 15.
[2] " De Ordine," i, 6.
[3] Ibid. i, 26.
[4] " Acad." ii, 10.
[5] Ibid. ii, 10.

Between Two Worlds

Augustine assures us that the books " Contra Academicos," " De Beata Vita," " De Ordine," do actually reproduce the substance of what was said by Licentius and Trygetius and, in the case of himself and Alypius, the very words.[1]

The Problem of Truth, the Problem of Happiness, these are what press upon them. We are discussing the same problems to-day with a very much larger apparatus of knowledge, psychological and historical, and a richer accumulation of the results of human thought. We cannot expect to find what these Roman Africans have to say about them in the year 386 very final or adequate. But they are the problems which lay deeper than the theological controversies which were to occupy the human mind so exclusively in the age to come. And now, as it were, before it determines to take so much for granted, before it shuts in its vision among those prepossessions, the human mind stands once more to take a free survey round about it ; it will recollect once more those searching critical questions, the inheritance of ancient thought after its long travail, before it surrenders itself altogether to this new thing which has arisen with a claim so tremendous and heart-subduing.

And if we are to bring the new thing into contact with the ancient thought where that thought is most searching, it will be less with its latest phase, the Neoplatonic, already full of adventurous beliefs, than with the older, more sceptical phase. We may be inclined less to ask : What was the attitude of Porphyry, say, to the system of Christian belief ? than : What would Carneades and the persistent doubters of the younger Academy have made of it? Well, these are just the people to whom Augustine at Casciago gives a hearing. Cicero had adhered to the Academy, it will be remembered, so far as he had adhered seriously to any school; a certain amount of his philosophical writing was actually a reproduction of Carneades in Latin; and Cicero had been the predominant philosophical influence of Augustine's early years. The first of those works which embody the conversations at Casciago bears the title "Contra Academicos."

"Do you doubt the proposition: We ought to know what is true (*verum nos scire oportere*)?" With such a question of Augustine's the series of conversations begins—uttered, we gather, at some pleasant spot near the house where the party has assembled, the *notarius* having his tablets or parchment ready. This leads to the question: Can the good of man be attained, or, in the phrase of those days, can a man have *vita beata* without a knowledge of the Truth? And here opposite views are maintained by Trygetius and Licentius. Trygetius holds that a knowledge of the Truth is essential to the *vita beata*; Licentius, that an honest search for the Truth suffices, whether it be found or not. He appeals to the authority of Carneades and Cicero in support of his contention. It is urged on the other side that a life which does not arrive at what it is seeking, obviously falls short of being *beata*; and we notice the axiom of ancient thought that any philosophy to be satisfactory must secure a good which is perfect in all respects. The Wise Man of the Stoics had to be absolutely free from defect or want; otherwise they felt a fatal flaw in their whole construction. This presupposition has often to be borne in mind while we follow these discussions.

"But the search, not the attainment," Licentius argues, may be the final good for man *in this life*. "That supreme Truth, I think, God alone knows, or may-be the human soul when it has left this dark prison-house of the body."[1] The seeker will be the perfect man, perfect *as man*. One may therefore reckon him *beatus*. But he finds it hard to meet the argument of Trygetius that the seeker is still in a condition of wandering (*error*) and that he who wanders (*errat*) cannot have attained happiness. He asks that the discussion may be adjourned till the morrow and the company consents.

"Then we arose to take a walk. We chatted about all sorts of things as we went, but Licentius remained plunged in thought. Finding this, however, bootless, he relaxed his mind and joined in our conversation. In the evening the two had fallen again into their argument; but I drew the line, and persuaded them to let the question stand over till another day. *Inde ad balneas.*"

Most of the following day is taken up with country things and the " Æneid," Book I, but late in the afternoon the discussion is renewed. Licentius has meanwhile seen light. *Errare* is obviously an ambiguous word. It may mean the accepting of what is false for true, or it may mean the withholding of any assent, the simple state of seeking; it is error in the former sense which is incompatible with *vita beata*, not error in the latter. " If any one is seeking Alexandria and making his way towards it by the right road, you cannot say that he is ' in error ' in the bad sense." Trygetius divines that the concep-

[1] i. 9.

tion of the *Wise Man* [1] traditional in ancient philosophy will prove his case that attainment is essential to *vita beata*. But this only opens the further question : What is *sapientia*? And ultimately the master, who is acting as umpire, has to be appealed to for a definition. But darkness has now fallen, and Augustine postpones his answer to the next day.

On this day the company has determined to leave plenty of time for philosophy, and the discussion is resumed soon after sunrise. Augustine declines to do more than give a bare definition of wisdom, and he chooses the old Stoic one, "the knowledge of things human and divine." This leads to a curious development of the argument. Is the knowledge of "things divine" (*res divinæ*) not exemplified in abnormal psychic perception? The ordinary usage of *divinus*, *divinatio*, suggested this. Albicerius, for instance, was a fashionable clairvoyant in Carthage a short while back. He performed some extraordinary feats. Flaccianus, after a business interview with somebody in the matter of a certain estate which he was purchasing, went to the clairvoyant and asked, "What have I just been doing?" Albicerius not only indicated the nature of the interview, but told him the name of the property involved, such an outlandish one that Flaccianus himself had hardly been able to remember it. Could Albicerius therefore be considered *sapiens*? His morals were flagitious. This ἀπορία is raised by Licentius, and Trygetius tries to expound the definition of *sapientia* in such a way as to make it fit his own ideal of the *sapiens*. The clairvoyants are ruled out, because the knowledge of divine things

[1] *Sapiens.*

implied by *sapientia* must be infallible, and the clair-voyants make as many misses as hits. Then the " knowledge of human things " means the knowledge of what really belongs to man as man, i.e. the four classical virtues—not my momentary thought of a verse, say, which the thought-reader can discover. The air all round us is no doubt full of demons, intelligences of a low order, without the Reason which is man's peculiar prerogative, although perhaps quicker and more subtle in perception, and by their means the psychic can get knowledge of certain matters—knowledge vastly inferior in value to the normal products of the human reason in the arts and sciences.

But if Albicerius is not *sapiens*, Licentius urges, the definition is too wide, since it seems an abuse of language to exclude *divinatio* from the *res divinæ*. Trygetius suggests it may be made closer by qualifying the human and divine things as those which belong to the *vita beata*. True as far as it goes, says Licentius, but now too narrow. The knowledge of such things is wisdom, but not the knowledge only, the diligent search after it as well.[1] The former constitutes the beatitude of God, the latter alone that of man in his present life. Before Trygetius can frame his answer, Augustine declares the session closed. He points out that one thing at any rate is acknowledged on both sides, the supreme value of Truth. The midday meal is now announced and all rise up.

After this a week goes by with no renewal of the dis-cussion. Then it is resumed one cloudless morning, when they have left the house early, Licentius asking Augustine to state the Academic, that is the Sceptical,

[1] i, 23.

position before they return for the midday meal. This
the master does along the lines familiar to the students
of ancient philosophy—the denial of any possibility of
arriving at certainty, the doctrine of the suspense of
judgement, and then, since some principle of action is
wanted, the doctrine that probability (the *veri simile*)
is the guide of life. They talk as they retrace their
steps to the house, and Alypius asks Augustine to define
the difference between the Old and New Academy. But
they are now at the door, and Monica uses gentle
violence to compel them to luncheon : " *Ita nos trudere
in prandium cœpit, ut verba faciendi locus non esset.*"

Luncheon over, the party returns to the meadow, and
Alypius, at Augustine's request, explains the position
of the New Academy in relation both to the Old
Academy and the still newer dogmatism of Antiochus.
Licentius, as spokesman for the Sceptical school, is now
pressed by Augustine. Does he hold that what the
Academics say is *true*? He sees the snare in time to
reply that it seems to him *probable*. But *probable* is
veri simile, and how can one know whether anything is
like Truth, if one does not know what Truth is ? [1]—as
if, Augustine says, some one, seeing your brother, should
remark that he is very like your father, when your father
is quite unknown to him ! This difficulty Licentius
cannot meet, and Trygetius comes to the rescue. But
against him too Augustine drives home the question,
How can one know what is *veri simile*, when one does
not know what is *verum* ? [2]

The defence of the Academic position is then thrown
upon Alypius, and the controversy proceeds between the

[1] ii, 16. [2] ii, 20.

master and his old friend. Augustine makes an interesting confession : he has not yet himself arrived at certainty ; only to him it appears probable that the Truth can be found by men.[1] The Academics hold that the probability is the other way ; that is the only difference between them. A little later he explains that he does not believe the Old Academic teachers to have been sceptics in reality, but to have made their scepticism a screen for concealing their true doctrine from the profane. He is prepared, however, to examine the sceptical position on its own merits—but not to-day, for the sun is low and it is time to go home.

Next day is another splendid summer day, but household affairs and the writing of letters do not leave them free till late in the afternoon. Then they wander out through the golden evening to the wonted tree. In the little space of daylight remaining the discussion meanders without bringing things much further. Only the declaration is obtained from Alypius that he himself holds that not only have men so far failed to find the Truth, but the Truth is unattainable ; the Academics accordingly in his view meant just what they said. This is what Augustine disputes, and the discussion is adjourned to the next day. The party returns home through the gathering shades of the mild night.

The fine weather does not last, and the following morning they meet, not in the meadow, but in the bath-hall of the country house. The search for Truth, the supreme business of life ! Once more the African master of rhetoric gives utterance to the passion which at this moment of his life has come to supersede all others—

[1] ii, 23.

the Truth, to which he feels himself now at last come so thrillingly near! And yet look at the hindrances, the pitiful necessities of life which seem to make the man who would live for Truth alone the slave of his material circumstances—of Fortune, in the ancients' manner of speaking. Think of yesterday, when we had to go to bed with our discussion adjourned, because mere household affairs took up so much of the day that we had only two short hours left over to pass into the sphere of our true being and breathe its free air (*in nosmetipsos respirare*).[1] It would almost seem as if, in order to reach the state of wisdom in which a man is independent of Fortune, the help of Fortune were required! Such an apparent paradox, however, Augustine reflects, has many parallels in common things: the ship which takes me across the Ægean enables me to reach a place where I require the ship no more. It may be so with the man who by Fortune's help reaches the haven of Wisdom. But this difference, in respect of independence of Fortune, between the state of the seeker and the state of the wise man Alypius is disposed to deny: if the wise man can in one sense do without Fortune, so can the seeker; if on the other hand the seeker needs Fortune for the maintenance of his bare physical life, so does the wise man. The question now supervenes, What is really the difference between the seeker and the wise man? The wise man possesses by a fixed disposition of soul (*habitus*) those things, says Alypius, for which the seeker has only a burning desire (*flagrantia*). And is it not, Augustine urges, just the Truth which the wise man possesses—the Truth whose unattainableness the Aca-

[1] iii, 2.

demic asserts ? Is it not an absurdity to say the wise man does not know wisdom ? Alypius would save the situation by the phrase, The wise man seems to himself to know wisdom. Augustine claims that this proves his case. If the wise man thinks that he knows wisdom he believes at any rate that the Truth is attainable.

They now break off for the midday meal. In the course of the meal Licentius slips away and is discovered afterwards in the bath-hall, absorbed in the composition of Greek tragic iambics—a display of literary ardour which the master can now only think dangerous to his soul, and Licentius is sent back to quench the literal physical thirst of which he has become aware, before the discussion is resumed.

Alypius before luncheon stated that the wise man thought that he knew wisdom. Well then, Augustine asks, what does Alypius himself think about him, that he knows wisdom or that he does not ? If the ideal wise man were found, Alypius opines, the wise man such as Reason presents him (*qualem ratio prodit*),[1] he might perhaps know. Augustine points out that this shifts the question from the Academic ground. The Academics held that the wise man was actually found, but that he never possessed real knowledge and never affirmed more than a probability. The position of Alypius is that wisdom would imply a knowledge of the Truth, but left us confronted with the question, Is the wise man ever found ? Granting that there is a Truth, not in its nature inaccessible, a Truth to which the wise man ought to give assent, who can point it out ? Alypius a moment before had drawn upon the myth of Proteus to figure

[1] iii, 9.

Hellenism and Christianity

this elusive Truth, so impossible to lay hold of, unless some divinity, as in the old story, showed the way (*nisi indice alicuius numinis*).[1] And now Augustine seizes upon the expression. Yes, that is where for him hope lies—an intimation conveyed from the other side, *numen aliquod!*

But before following up that clue, Augustine turns to examine the Academic position by the light of reason. This part of his argument, it must be allowed, is directed against a position which we should hardly feel it worth while to assail so elaborately. The kind of sceptic which we want him to meet is not the extreme sceptic who denies that we can know any proposition whatever to be true—but the sceptic who asks Augustine's ground for believing those particular things about the unseen Reality which he has found taught in the Christian community. It is comparatively easy to show the absurdity of the extreme sceptical position, but that does not take us all the way to accepting the Christian belief. It is, however, against the extreme position that Augustine argues. If we assert that we can make no proposition with the assurance of its truth, our very assertion is an instance to the contrary; this, of course, was the stock argument against the Sceptics. Or again, disjunctive propositions must be true: the World is either one or it is not one, and so on. Thirdly, the external world surrounding me may be an illusion; I may be mad or dreaming; but the fact that something appears to me, that there is an It about which I can speak, remains indubitable. Fourthly, mathematical truths must be true, even if I am dreaming: six and

[1] iii, 11.

one make seven, whatever my condition is. Fifthly, I know the quality of my sensations as sensations, whatever their external cause may be : I *do* see the straight staff bent in a pool ; I *do* taste the leaves of the wild olive as bitter, whatever they may be to goats. And with this Augustine seems to connect, sixthly, moral judgments.[1] "*Quid enim de moribus inquirentem iuvat vel impedit corporis sensus ?*" Even the Epicureans are not prevented by the deceitfulness of the senses from knowing what excites pleasure in them and what dislike—from making value-judgements, in the cant phrase of modern philosophy. But may I not be dreaming all the while when I choose my *summum bonum* ? Then my choosing it will not matter, for my choice will all be part of the dream. Seventhly and lastly, Augustine points to "dialectic," i.e. formal logic, as something which the wise man, if it is true, will know for certain. This last instance, of course, is, in substance, identical with that of disjunctive propositions already given. The argument of Alypius that the very victory of Augustine over the Academics would prove that the acutest and most brilliant philosophers could be mistaken and therefore signally confirm the sceptical doubt,[2] Augustine meets by saying that he is willing to waive his victory, if only he can remove the despair which paralyses the search for Truth at the outset ; and once more he returns to his contention that the knowledge of wisdom is involved in the idea of the wise man.

All this, however, is to move in an abstract formal region without coming near any concrete truth. Augustine himself feels that it cannot satisfy. " Perhaps," he

[1] iii, 27. [2] iii, 30.

says,[1] " you want me to quit my logical fortress and come to close quarters with the shrewd adversary. I will, to please you. I will throw with all the power I possess a dart, smoky indeed and uncouth, but, as I think, effective. To abstain from all assent is to forgo all activity. They smile contemptuously. ' *O hominem rusticum !* What of our *probabile* ? What of our *veri simile* ? ' There ! I have done as you wished ; and you hear the ring of the Greek shields. My poor dart has been intercepted ; I look in vain for help to the old learned books. The armour with which they provide me is rather a burden than an aid. I will turn to what these green fields, this country quiet, have taught me. Yes, in these long unhurried summer and autumn days, here among meadows and woods, I have been thinking deeply what power lies in that *probabile* to save our activities from error. It seemed at first such a sound and adequate security, not a crack anywhere. And then gradually I began to see a gap in my defences. Suppose two way-farers bound for the same place come to a parting of the ways. They stand in doubt which is the right road, when a shepherd comes upon the scene. ' Good day, my worthy man (*Salve, frugi homo*), tell us, please, which is the way to such-and-such a place ? ' ' Follow this road, and ye won't go wrong.' ' He has told us true,' says one wayfarer to his fellow, ' let us go as he says.' But the other wayfarer is a sceptical philosopher, and highly amused at any one giving his assent so easily. While the simple man goes on, he remains rooted at the cross-roads. He is beginning to feel his position rather ridiculous, when down the other road some one comes

[1] iii, 33.

Between Two Worlds

into view—not a shepherd this time, but a sleek man of fashion on horseback (*lautus et urbanus quidam*). The philosopher asks him the way, and, in order to enlist the interest of some one so obviously a member of the polite world, indicates the philosophical nature of the considerations which have immobilized him where he stands. Unfortunately the brilliant gentleman is really a sharper (a *samardacus* in fourth-century slang) and deliberately directs him to the wrong road. This indication the philosopher follows ; but is he deceived ? Not in the least ; all the way that he goes he repeats to himself that he is only following the probable ; he has never given his absolute intellectual assent. The simple man, who gave his assent rashly, arrives happily at his destination, and the cautious philosopher loses himself, still following the probable, in far-off forests."

Now, according to the Academics the man who took the right road by a happy chance must be said to be in error, and the philosopher who gets lost not to be in error. This seemed to Augustine so monstrous a conclusion that he began to suspect the basis of the Academic doctrine. Perhaps we of the twentieth century, listening to the discussion, would object at this point that Augustine's parable does not really touch the doctrine that probability is the guide of life. Of course, we should say, man is always liable to make a mistake, but that is no reason for our following blindly the shepherd's instructions any more than the fine gentleman's. If we make a mistake, we shall by following rational probability have done the best we could. Ah ! but that is just what neither side in the ancient controversy was willing to admit. The wise man, on this the schools were agreed, must be one who made no mistake. And the Academics thought they saved this postulate by their doctrine that the wise man withheld absolute intellectual assent, and was therefore not in error even if his action turned out to be futile. Now, against this position Augustine's argument seems to have force. The only real suspense of judgement, it would say in effect, is suspense of action. All action involves assent. It is small good saying that this is not absolute intellectual assent, if the action turns out to be wrong.

Augustine now proceeds to the moral consequences of the Academic theory. They are, of course, a subjectivism of the most extreme form. All the moral judgements of society, all the legal penalties attached to crime, are based upon the belief that there is an objective right and wrong. If the Academics are right, they are all stultified. This is a theme which lends itself to rhetorical expansion. One has only to take examples of crime, a man seducing his friend's wife, Catiline—" *taceo de homicidiis, parricidiis, sacrilegiis,*" and so on, asking sarcastically after each, whether there was here no fault (*peccatum*), no error, because the criminal was following the course which commended itself to him personally. To us the rhetoric adds little to whatever force the argument may have.

Augustine has now proved to his own satisfaction that *some* truth at any rate is accessible to men. The extreme sceptical position has been shown untenable. That position, however, he now goes on to expound, was never really held by the Academics. The Platonic Academia was a society with an esoteric doctrine incapable of being transmitted to the profane, and the profane

Between Two Worlds

par excellence were the materialist Stoics. The Academic Scepticism did a necessary work of destruction upon the Stoic dogmas. Cicero gave them the *coup de grâce.* " Within a little of his time the stubborn opposition was extinct : the pure and luminous face of Plato shone forth clear of the mists of error which had hidden it, most chiefly in Plotinus, a Platonic philosopher who has been held so like the master that one might have supposed the two to have lived together, whilst so long an interval of time in fact separated them that the master might be thought to have come to life again in Plotinus." [1] This is hardly how we should have expected Augustine to express himself a few months after his conversion, if we only knew his life from the " Confessions."

And now we see how the Christian belief has been grafted on to a Platonic stock.[2] " At the present time," Augustine goes on, " all schools of philosophy are practically extinct except the Cynics, the Peripatetics, and the Platonists. The Cynics may be dismissed as freaks, and as to Plato and Aristotle, it is only the dull or careless who do not see that there is a profound underlying agreement between them in doctrine and moral ideals. So that after the strifes and controversies of ages now at last, I think, a uniform teaching embodying a supremely true philosophy has been strained out (*eliquata est*)—a philosophy ' not of this world ' "—Augustine is quoting the Christian scriptures, but he gives the phrase a curious Platonic twist—" not of this material world, but of the other world of the mind (*alterius intelligibilis*)." But how is the soul, darkened with the manifold clouds of error, besmirched deep in its being with the pollutions

[1] iii, 41.　　　　　　　　[2] iii, 42.

of the body, to rise to the mind-world (the νοητὸς κόσμος) ?
The old Platonic question ; but it gets no longer a
Platonic answer. This is where the Christianity in this
strange combination comes in. It could not rise, had not
the supreme God " by a kind of popular clemency (*populari
quadam clementia*) " lowered the authority of the Divine
Intellect even to a human body ; so that now souls can
be roused up, not only by His instructions, but by His
acts, and return to their true selves and see again
their lost country, without the dust and tumult of
controversy.

In a few concluding sentences Augustine states his
own personal standpoint at that moment of time : so
did a man reason in the year 386, suspended between the
ancient world that was passing away and the new world
gradually coming to be. " Wherever human wisdom
may lie, I Augustinus have not yet apprehended it.[1]
But I am only thirty-two and need not despair. My
whole life is henceforward to be concentrated upon the
search for it, all the things that men count good
sacrificed to that one end. It was the Academic arguments which discouraged me at the very outset, but they
at any rate have been disposed of. And now what are
the forces which draw the mind to learn, which condition
its receptivity ? They are two, authority and reason.
As for the first, I have made up my mind to stand by
the authority of Christ ; for I find in the world none
stronger. As for the second—because I am eager to
understand as well as believe—I feel sure that I shall
find among the Platonists all the truth that can be
attained by the subtlest reason, and these I shall follow

[1] iii, 43.

so long as their teaching does not conflict with our religion.''

Night has already fallen, and the lamps were brought in some while since to enable the shorthand-writer to take his notes. The voice we have been listening to ceases, and we find ourselves back again in the present year of our Lord, still looking out upon this old problematic universe.

VII

THE PROPHET OF PERSONALITY

WHILST every year fresh annotated editions of the masterpieces bequeathed us by the " classical " period of Greek and Latin literature pour from the presses of Europe, Dr. Pusey's edition of the " Confessions " of Augustine (1838) was the solitary annotated text published in England till the Cambridge University Press published an edition (by Dr. Gibb and Dr. Montgomery) in 1908. How far this striking disproportion is due to an antiquated superstition which set the productions of certain limited periods upon an unapproachable eminence, how far it is merely due to the requirements of secondary education, one need not inquire. The disproportion remains striking. There seems no rational principle of valuation which would make the " Confessions " less classical, whether in respect of their intrinsic power or their actual normative effect in thought and literature, than the writings of Cicero. And it is perhaps worth considering whether the traditional lines drawn in our system of classical education have any real sense left. The Latin of Augustine is, of course, no more identical with the Latin of Cicero than the English of Carlyle is with the English of Hooker. And in days when the object of a classical

The Prophet of Personality

education was to enable men to write a Latin of the precise Ciceronian complexion, something might be said for not confusing a learner's ideals by acquainting him with the masters of another style. But since the educators of to-day take the main object of a classical education to be, not so much to impart an elegant accomplishment, as to enable those whom they teach to enter upon the great inheritance of thought and expression embodied in the dead tongues, one might raise the question whether a more liberal range of Latin reading in our schools would not be justified. Some precision in the discrimination of " classical " forms might be lost ; but would not such loss, in the case of the ordinary man, be more than made up for by an enrichment of vital interests ? What a part the Latin Bible has played in the world ! How its phrases shaped thought and expression in the birth of our modern literatures ! Would not a greater appreciation of this side of our Latin heritage compensate for some " barbarisms " in the Latin prose of a boy who learnt the language, not in order to become a philological specialist, but in order to understand better the world we live in ? For the specialist the standard of linguistic discrimination might remain as high, as exacting, as ever.

If what gives any writer or any age the right to " classical " rank is language used effectively as the vehicle of such thought or feeling as has a permanent interest for mankind, then there is no reason, except an academic convention, to give the writing of Cicero a higher value than that of Augustine. Latin was still, in the Africa of A.D. 400, a living tongue which could modify itself to express a new world of thoughts and feelings. And how far a traditional medium can be modified and enriched for the expression of new ideas we can never tell till the masters arise, in whom those ideas demand expression. The Latin of Cicero was to some extent his own creation for the expression of Greek philosophy; and in the four centuries between Cicero and Augustine how much had come into the world! We should perhaps never have dared to forecast how this speech of massive construction, made, it would seem, for rock-graven epigram or magisterial formula, could be used to convey the outpouring of mystical devotion, to catch the elusive quality of shadowy moods, to enter into the subtleties of psychological analysis. Think, for instance, of the difficulties presented in this field by a language which was without a definite article, which could only represent " the Good," " the Beautiful " (τὸ ἀγαθόν, τὸ καλόν), by an equivalent either cumbrous or obscure. Virgil indeed had brought out new faculties in Latin for emotional suggestion, and Virgil, we know, had entered more than any other old Latin writer into the fabric of Augustine's soul.

And with what masterful boldness Augustine handles the ancestral language! Much indeed of the novelty is due to a stream of literary tradition, wholly strange to Cicero, having mingled with the Latin of the schools—the Hebraic tradition which had come in with the Latin Bible. The purity of the Latin idiom, it may be said, was spoilt by the alien influx; the Latin of the *Vetus Itala* is not Latin at all. But what language has not been modified—why should we not say enriched?—by foreign influences? Had not the speech of the old Roman burgess been shaped to literary uses by the influence of Greek? Was not classical

The Prophet of Personality

Latin poetry at its beginning an exotic, which supplanted the old native systems of verse ? The language which Augustine found in his Latin Psalter gave a vehicle of expression to the emotions of the New Life, emotions so elementary and so profound, such as was not offered by any language of the approved academic pattern. And language drawn directly from the Biblical writings, or caught from their influence, came instinctively to his lips as his soul rose in confession or adoration or prayer.

Qui novit veritatem, novit eam [the spiritual Light], et qui novit eam, novit æternitatem. Caritas novit eam ! O æterna veritas et vera caritas et cara æternitas ! Tu es Deus meus, tibi suspiro die ac nocte.

How far we have travelled from Cicero ! Not that the language of such a passage as this is purely scriptural. The scriptural element is obvious, but it has been taken up and fused in the fire of one ardent and intense personality with the ideals in which the long search of ancient philosophy had ended. Where Augustine is concerned, less with direct devotion than with descriptive psychology, the Hebraic idiom did not offer the same means of expression. Here Augustine was thrown upon the resources of his own vivid genius. And how enormously the Christian's perception of the psychological problem went beyond the wisdom of the ancient schools ! How much that had once seemed so easy to read off, so distinct and simple and classifiable, was found to be dim and complicated and infinitely mysterious ! " The abysmal depths of personality "—it was Augustine who first gave men an inkling of what that meant. The very phrase is his —" abyssus humanæ conscientiæ." " Est aliquid hominis quod nec ipse scit spiritus hominis, qui in ipso est,"

Hellenism and Christianity

" A man comprises something which not even the spirit of the man, which is in him, knows." Is not this a truth which modern developments of psychology have more and more tended to unfold ? Of descriptive psychology Augustine may be said to be the father. No one before had turned his eye inwards with such inquiring interest and steady purpose. The analysis of mood and motive which makes up a substantial part of the " Confessions " is still fresh and illuminating to-day after all that has been achieved by our modern psychological novelists in the way of subtle observation. It is almost superfluous to point to the particular passages in the book, which will occur to every one who knows it at all ; perhaps passages like those which deal with the psychology of childhood, or with the moods which follow upon bereavement,[1] or with the inward battle of wills,[2] one feels to be the most epoch-making. And Augustine's power of observation is matched by his power to coin the appropriate phrase. " In ictu trepidantis aspectus," he says of the flash of spiritual vision ; " in aula ingenti memoriæ meæ," " sero te amavi, pulchritudo tam antiqua et tam nova, sero te amavi ! " These are the kind of things one does not easily forget. " Quicquid aspiciebam mors erat," he says, to describe the horror of his first great bereavement, hitting upon almost the same form of expression as a living French writer chooses, when he has to express a similar experience: " Le soleil d'Octobre . . . je sens de la mort, de la mélancolie de mort, dans sa lumière douce ; ses rayons sont pleins de mort."

[1] Book IV.
[2] The great garden scene of Book VIII.

The Prophet of Personality

It was a great discovery this—of what men had been wanting so long without knowing it, the story of the heart. They had indeed been always, as Augustine calls them, " curiosum genus ad cognoscendam vitam alienam," and yet the classical writers had persisted in the supposition that it was only the loud actions of court and assembly and battlefield, or the pure industry of the intellect, or at any rate passion in its most obvious animal forms, which interested them. " Personality "—has some one not said that ?—was never distinctly conceived of by antiquity. And yet by personality men had been secretly governed all the time. And when Augustine unfolded before them a history of things not seen with the eyes, of battles waged without sound, of a kingdom that came not with observation, his book took the world by storm. It won a place immediately among the normative influences in men's minds, which it has not lost, even among the multitudinous literature of to-day. The great masters of antiquity had bequeathed splendid memorials of what they thought ; they had transmitted little to show what they were. If we had to find any parallel in pre-Christian antiquity to this influence of a man prolonged to later generations by the image of his personality, contained in his writings, we should perhaps have to find it in a quarter very ill-seen by all serious people in the time of Augustine—in the influence which Epicurus had long exercised in his school, where personal admiration of the Master counted for so much. In his letters, if we may judge by what is left, he still lived ; in the famous one penned on the threshold of death a drama of the soul was presented, whose power over men we can still understand—" bodily torments continuous, so great that they exhaust all possibilities of pain, but, against them all, the joy in the soul standing unvanquished, when I call to mind our conversations of old."

But it was the experiences of the New Life which really broke up the lower depths, which gave a novel interest to that which went on in the mysterious region of emotion and will. Simply as a phenomenon in literature, the letters of Paul are of immense significance. No earlier writing that we possess gives a revelation of any man's personality so penetrating and so profound. And the direct influence of Paul is one of the capital moments in Augustine's development. The famous description of the conflict of wills in the garden is an expansion of Romans vii. If Augustine did not take up into his thought the whole teaching of Paul, no Christian teacher since the early days had come so near to understanding and reproducing the Apostle.

As an original thinker Augustine has been a determining force in European history. He stood on the confines of the ancient and medieval worlds. He was, in a manner, a child of the old philosophic tradition, and had, by his own confession, come to Christ by way of Cicero and Plotinus. Neo-platonism he took over almost bodily, considering it a sort of inchoate Christianity. At the same time he was the fashioner of a great part of Catholic theology ; yes and also, in Harnack's phrase, " the first modern man."

How far, it is asked, is the picture drawn by Augustine in the " Confessions " of his conversion to Christ true to fact ? How far is it distorted and miscoloured in his later memory ? What creates the difficulty is the very different impression given by those writings of Augustine, including letters to intimate friends, which belong in date to the first years of his Christian profession. Instead of the agonies of soul-searching and contrition, instead of the violent break with old interests, which one gathers from the " Confessions," his earliest writings and letters, it is urged, show him genially cultivating Latin literature and Neoplatonic philosophy, with a Christianity only of the most shadowy sort. His real conversion to Christianity did not, according to this view, take place till a considerable time after the experience from which his life in Christ is ordinarily dated.

The strength of the argument depends upon its taking the contemporary account of his feelings and standpoint to be fairly complete and transparent. And considering the private letters, we must probably admit that the account in the " Confessions " is somewhat idealized in retrospect. On the other hand, the extreme view does not seem to allow enough for the extent to which a conventional mode of expression may create an opacity which conceals the heart. Even in writing to his friends Augustine may well have been more or less dominated for some time by the forms of expression which were regarded as proper to cultured society. Much that lay deep might only discover itself later on, as an utterance more violent and direct broke through the traditional forms.

And yet, when all is said and done, it remains true that as time went on, Augustine saw all that belonged to his old life in ever blacker colours. In his earliest Christian writings he still had words of warm admiration for his first teacher, Cicero, and he would spend a morning over Virgil. In the " Confessions " Cicero is spoken of

Hellenism and Christianity

with cold aloofness, " Cicero quidam," and what allusions there are to the " Æneid " are contemptuous. In his book " Against the Academics " he composes a pretty little parable of the kinship of Philosophy and Art (Philocalia) ; in the " Retractions " he passes over it a remorseless hand of condemnation—" prorsus inepta et insulsa fabula "—Art, being concerned with material things, is concerned with trash. More and more the many colours of life seemed to him only an undesirable stain upon the white radiance of eternity. He reproaches himself because his thought has been distracted by the sight of a hare running or a spider catching flies. He suffers agonies of shame and contrition because he cannot eat after fasting without some gust of sensual pleasure.

Contrast this line of Augustine's development with that which the autobiographic record shows in the case of another religious leader, John Wesley. To the expressions of uncompromising condemnation which Wesley had passed upon his earlier life at the time of his great critical experience, he appends later on, in the light of mature experience, comments gently mitigating or qualifying. We find him occasionally go on his preaching tours accompanied by a volume of Ariosto. Augustine's asceticism was, in truth, not purely Christian ; it was breathed in from an atmosphere impregnated with Neo-platonism and Oriental dualism. Yet the asceticism is only one element in a character whose self-revelation will always appeal to mankind, a character in which the Christian recognizes, through whatever refractions of the particular human medium, the fire of the One Spirit.

VIII

DIRT

WE are not accustomed to associate the idea of dirt with anything so honourable as philosophy, yet experience has often shown that it is just the thing lying, as the Greek phrase is, " before the foot," which it is hardest to take account of, and perhaps the philosopher may find that the dirt actually adhering to his foot, as he walks the miry ways of the world, starts him, if he considers of it curiously, upon a train of reflections which will carry him far. Let him but begin by asking the simple question, What is dirt ? The popular answer (fathered sometimes upon the poet Southey, sometimes upon Palmerston), " Matter in the wrong place," plainly does not help us much. If all dirt is matter in the wrong place, there is a great deal of matter in the wrong place, which is not dirt—the books upon my shelf after they have been taken out and replaced by a housemaid, my watch in the pocket of a thief, my body if I mistake the train at a railway junction. But this is perhaps to insist upon the obvious. Even if by " matter " we mean minute particles of matter, and if by its being in a " wrong place " we mean its adhering to a foreign body from which, for some human purpose, it were better away, our definition is still too wide. I should not regard my food as " dirty," because it was too strongly peppered, nor should I put a poisonous powder into the category of " dirt." And if the field of the disagreeable and the noxious extends in one direction beyond that of the polluting, it is equally true that we regard a good deal as dirt, which we could not show to be particularly noxious or painful. The two fields overlap, but they do not coincide. And even if they overlap in their *denotation*, to use the old terms of Formal Logic, the *connotation* of the term " noxious " seems wholly different from that of the term " polluting." The feeling which leads a man to object to being spat upon is not simply that he calculates a certain risk of infection by another man's saliva.

The idea of dirt seems to imply a special feeling of repugnance or indignity—a repugnance, a sense of indignity, *sui generis*, not identical with the shrinking from the dangerous, for instance, or even from the ugly. The feeling seems to take class among the elementary constituents of human mentality, like the sense of moral value or the sense of beauty. All attempts to define it seem to beg the very notion to be defined, the idea of pollution. Now, even if we had no other interest in it, an elementary constituent of this sort must interest the moral philosopher by the very analogy it offers to the sense of moral value. Here, too, the error can be illustrated of confusing the question of origins with the question of value. Just as we can trace the development of morality from embryonic beginnings among primitive superstitions, just as we can classify the various things which in various ages have been held right or

Dirt

wrong, and yet leave untouched the question what "right" and "wrong" *mean*, what value belongs to the whole process of development, what insight moral valuation gives into Reality, so, in the case of dirt, we can trace, it may be, the connexion between our own feelings and primitive taboos or old religious laws of ceremonial cleanness ; but that does not tell us what cleanness and pollution *are*, or whether there is anything real corresponding to the mass of feelings which those terms connote for us.

It seems arguable, for instance, that the feeling of dirt is developed as a protection against noxious germs before the presence of such germs could be detected by bacteriological science ; that the notion of uncleanness was at the beginning only a crude semi-superstitious way by which primitive man warded off disease and sepsis. If so, it might seem that, as super-stition gave way to reason, the whole notion of dirt, uncleanness, pollution, would disappear from the human mind, having fulfilled its function. Man would still avoid certain forms of matter, as liable to harbour disease germs, but he would avoid them for purely prudential reasons, without any of that feeling of moral unworth, that instinctive emotional recoil, which his ancestors had associated with the idea of being dirty. Such a view might find support in the consideration that, as a matter of fact, the progress of civilization has eliminated the notion of uncleanness in reference to many objects regarded as unclean by primitive or by medieval man. I was once told a story by a friend of mine, an Anglo-Indian official, which seems to me extremely suggestive in this connexion. The Englishman had engaged a worthy

Hellenism and Christianity

Mohammedan *munshi* to teach him the vernacular, with whom he came to have very friendly and confidential relations. But one day his teacher came to him with a face of horror; he had, he said, just been told something about the sahibs so disgusting that he could not believe it. A friend had assured him that they habitually put into their *mouths* the bone of a dog with the bristles of a pig. Was this true? The Englishman had to admit that it was undoubtedly true. He went on, of course, to explain that the process by which toothbrushes were prepared insured that both the bone and the bristles were free from noxious or offensive matter. But it was useless. The fact remained for the Indian that the object was—what it was. The instinct by which he recoiled from it was not affected by the proof that it was innocuous. He could never after that disguise a feeling of constraint and repugnance in his intercourse with my friend, as with a person of unspeakably filthy habits.

We are ready enough to smile at such a scruple, because it seems to have no basis in reason. What, however, may give us pause is to ask whether our own application of the category of dirt has a basis in reason—whether the same progress of civilization which has made the feeling of the Mohammedan seem to us childish and superstitious may not make our own scruples seem childish and superstitious to generations more perfectly rationalized. And when we examine our feeling, as it actually exists, it seems to show those very contradictions which appear to us so strange in primitive superstition. Anthropologists often point out that two notions which to us seem diametrically opposed—that of *sacred* and of

Dirt

unclean—tend with primitive man to coalesce. " The conceptions of holiness and pollution are not yet differentiated in his mind. To him the common feature of these persons is that they are dangerous and in danger, and the danger in which they stand and to which they expose others is what we should call spiritual or supernatural. To seclude these persons from the rest of the world so that the dreaded spiritual danger shall neither reach them nor spread from them is the object of the taboos which they have to observe. These taboos act, so to say, as electrical insulators to preserve the spiritual force with which these persons are charged from suffering or inflicting harm by contact with the outer world." [1] A curious instance among peoples even of advanced civilization is the phrase current among the rabbis to express the sanctity of the canonical scriptures, that they " defile the hands."

Now is this contradiction any more strange than those involved in the complex of instincts covered by our conception of dirt, though we do not reflect upon them enough to be aware of the inconsistency ? The holiest thing, to our instinctive feeling, is surely the mouth. There is nothing that we protect so jealously from contact with pollution. When we think of any object as unclean, no idea could provoke such horror and disgust as that of putting it into our mouth. And yet that which comes out of the mouth communicates special defilement ; the saliva retained without any sense of pollution in the holy place is unclean as soon as it is ejected. Probably the great majority of people of fastidious habits would

[1] Sir J. G. Frazer, " The Golden Bough " (First edition), i, pp. 171, 172.

feel that water into which they had washed their teeth was unclean, not for others only, but for themselves ; they would much rather put their hands into water in which another man had washed his hands before them than into water into which they had rinsed their own mouths. It would perhaps be as difficult to find a basis in reason for this feeling as for the Indian's feeling about tooth-brushes.

Whether, then, our feeling about dirt is a survival of primitive superstition, or whether it has something of absolute moral value, on either theory surely this complex of instincts offers the philosopher something of singular interest. If it be a mere survival, it is indeed destined to disappear with the advance of rational civilization. The field of the unclean, which now overlaps with the field of the noxious, will cease to exist and leave the field of the noxious subsisting alone. Men of future generations will understand perfectly, if they are told that contact with certain forms of matter involves a risk of disease, and they will be proportionately annoyed or alarmed if they come into conflict with them inadvertently. But they will never feel " dirty." They will not know what " dirty " means. But, if this is so, how interesting to the philosopher to find this mass of irrational primitive feeling still here in such force to-day, here in the full daylight, as we are apt to conceive it, of rational civilization ! To the student who desires to enter into those forms of primitive mentality, that network of taboos, which anthropologists report to us, and which are often so hard for us to construe, how important that he has here in his own world, in his own mind, something of the same quality !

Dirt

But is the feeling a mere survival? The other possible theory—that it belongs to the perfection of human nature, like the sense of moral obligation or the sense of beauty, makes it still more interesting to the philosopher. Perhaps it is arguing in a circle to appeal to the testimony of moral feeling, as it exists to-day, in support of this view. And yet we may, I think, take account of the strength with which our moral feeling seems to affirm a principle of absolute validity somewhere in our sense of dirt. This sense is found to be associated pre-eminently with excrements. It is probably because it is a secretion that saliva, as was noted above, although coming from the holy place, conveys pollution. The feeling as to the uncleanness of excrements goes far beyond any logically drawn conclusion from their dangerousness as breeders of disease, and seems, if reflected upon, to lead us to the mystical threshold. May not this sense of the unparalleled uncleanness of that which proceeds from the body be somehow connected, in the dim ground of things, by that strange association of the holy and the unclean, with the holiness of the body? If we can conceive some stronger race of men coming in upon our Western world, as Europeans have come in upon the East, men beyond us in scientific attainment, in command over the forces of Nature, in the practical intellect, should we not nevertheless feel a horror of them, as unspeakably unclean, if they were eaters of excrements? And would that feeling of repulsion be merely like the feeling of the Indian Mohammedan as to the use of bone toothbrushes (we should certainly appear to them as the *munshi* appeared to my Anglo-Indian friend), or would it be true that at this point our sensibility raised us above them, that what they had lost and we retained was an element in human nature of eternal value?

If those philosophers are right who see in Reason, in the sense of moral value, in the sense of beauty, an unfolding of the mind of God within the spirit of man (and to this view those of us who are Christians must adhere), must we not also hold that our sense of clean and unclean has its ground in the Divine Reality—that there are things really unclean " in the sight of God " ? And here the philosopher must take note that the relation of the moral sense and the sense of dirt is not only one of analogy, as we have considered it so far, but that the connexion is something much closer. For in all ages, among all peoples, wrong-doing has itself been felt to be a kind of pollution; uncleanness is one of the aspects of sin. And if, as has been argued, the sense of clean and unclean is a fundamental element of the human mind, one may express some surprise that the philosophers have given it so little consideration, in treating the moral problem. They seem to take the moral sense too exclusively as a sense of obligation, and the mental disquiet occasioned by wrong-doing as only a consciousness of obligation violated. They seem hardly to have tried to fathom the significance of that constant association in popular language of sin and uncleanness. The man who is sorry for having done wrong does not only feel that he has violated an obligation; he feels unclean.

Of course there is a special class of sins with which the feeling of pollution is pre-eminently associated. For the universality of this association we can again appeal to common language. It is not only in circles influenced by Christianity that indulgence of the sexual instinct

Dirt

is regarded as uncleanness, impurity in a peculiar sense. Words like " spurcus ," " immundus " had such special meaning long before they passed into Christian use. The Greeks, it is true, preferred characteristically to express their feeling of repugnance to such transgressions as a sense of *ugliness* (αἰσχρότης, αἰσχροποιῶ, etc.), rather than a sense of *defilement*. But the underlying feeling was the same. One finds sometimes the custom of sacred prostitution, existing at certain Hellenic shrines, pointed to as evidence that the ancient Greek had not our sense of an uncleanness attaching to such practices, and much is made of the fact that Pindar composed a *skolion* in honour of the πολύξεναι νεάνιδες of Corinth. Yet this very poem is, as a matter of fact, evidence that a brand of indignity was already fixed by the conscience of the day upon the occupation of these unhappy creatures. For the poet himself is not at ease. " I wonder," he admits frankly, " what the lords of the Isthmus will say of me, devising such inception of a honey-sweet *skolion* in connexion with public women." Those who refer to the poem often take no account of these significant words.

Here again we are brought to the close association of uncleanness with sanctity. For it is the same act which in one mental context is the very type of impurity and in another context is the sacrament of love and life. It would seem as if some slight change in circumstances could transfer its character straight away from one end of the moral scale to the other. Can a thing pass by so rapid a transition into its opposite ? In the sphere of the logical reason, perhaps no. The opinion directly contrary to the one I hold is the last you can bring me to.

Hellenism and Christianity

But the feeling of sanctity and uncleanness belongs to the sphere of the emotions, and in the sphere of the emotions it is the opposites which are joined by a close and subtle connexion. Love and hate are opposites, and yet it has been often observed that one passes more easily into the other than either into indifference. The basis of both is an interest concentrated upon a particular person, which may take on one character or the other, but cannot be characterless. A certain gamut of emotions, we might express it in the figurative style of modern psychology, has become intensely active and the mind may oscillate up and down it. Unlike as the two ends are, they agree in belonging to that particular line, and, when any part of the line is excited, the two ends are more closely connected with each other than with anything lying outside the line altogether. Just so in the case of sanctity; a certain group of emotions with regard to a particular object becomes active. We feel something thrilling about it; we have to overcome an inner shrinking in coming near to it; but according to circumstances the feeling may be that it is peculiarly holy, or that it is peculiarly unclean.

Deep at the bottom of all our sense of uncleanness, of dirt, is the feeling, primitive, irresolvable, universal, of the sanctity of the body. Nothing in the material sphere can properly be dirty except the body. We speak of a " dirty road," but in an uninhabited world moist clay would be no more dirty than hard rock; it is the possibility of clay adhering to a foot which makes it mire. A dwelling-place is dirty when it is in a state to communicate defilement to the bodies moving about in it; a plate is dirty when it may attach unworthy matter to that

Dirt

which, as food, is to enter the holy place. To discover this law written in the hearts of all men is to enter the region of a sane and strong mysticism. For the mysticism of the higher sort is not that which finds its count in the abnormal and extravagant, but that which discovers the mystery in the heart of the normal and universal. " To see a world in a grain of sand, and heaven in a wild flower "—but, most of all, to find in the ordinary working of the human personality something transcendent. The principle at work in our moral sense, in our sense of beauty, is not something unreasonable in the wide acceptation of the word Reason, sanctioned by Idealist philosophy, but it is something beyond the reach of reason, in the sense of argument or demonstration—to make the distinction upon which a friend of mine, now gone hence, Charles Keary, insisted in his finely written book " The Pursuit of Reason." And another of these laws written upon the heart seems to be this of the sanctity of the body. Here, too, we have a sense of worth and unworth, which we cannot argue about or justify logically, but which is simply there. And men professing to care for nothing but what is clear and demonstrable, based upon palpable scientific fact, men to whom everything that savours of mysticism, metaphysics, or religion, is at once ruled out, will yet pay strange unconscious homage to these instincts of the deeper soul. They will experience a peculiar mental discomfort, it may be, if, glancing down at their own hand, they see that the nails are black —not because they fear any contagion, not even because they see a combination of colours which is ugly in itself, but because they feel somehow desecrated in body by the alien particles adhering to the holy thing.

Hellenism and Christianity

This feeling about the body, no doubt, goes to explain why carnal sins have always seemed "impure" in a special sense. And it is perhaps well to understand that feelings are involved in this matter which lie deeper than the sphere of argument. In these days one finds people who speak and write as if the relation of the sexes were something that could be put on a plain, scientific, common-sense basis, without any mystery or sentiment or hocus-pocus of that sort. Proceeding by the way of matter-of-fact argument, they are perhaps for making bold changes in the code which regulates this relation in the society round about them. Well, there is no human code, one may agree, but is always liable to be found inadequate by the upward-struggling spirit of man. Yet let us remember that it was not only processes of overt reasoning which went to the making of that code, but that dim instincts of all sorts helped to shape it—some, it may be, low and self-regarding, the outcome of transient social conditions, but some deliverances of the inner oracle in man's heart. And if the code is to undergo change, it is not logical argument alone which can guide the general judgement ; the instincts of the deeper soul, the deeper spiritual reason, must have their part. And may we not say that the deeper reason has not left itself without witness in a sphere seemingly the most common, the most earthy, that we acknowledge its authority, blindly it may be, every time we utter the word "dirt"?

IX

A PARADOX OF CHRISTIANITY

CHRISTIANITY is the religion of cheerfulness. Its Founder was known for His delight in the lilies of the field, birds, and little children. The sunshine was dear to Him. It was all part of the large kindness of the Heavenly Father, bestowed upon the unthankful and the evil no less than upon the righteous. " Rejoice in the Lord always, and again I say, Rejoice," wrote the apostle Paul. One of the most striking characteristics of the primitive Christian community, in contrast with the surrounding heathen world, Freiherr von Dobschütz tells us, was its extraordinary happiness. " Ye rejoice," one of its members wrote to his friends, " with joy unspeakable and full of glory." " Put away therefore from thyself," wrote another, " sadness, and afflict not the Holy Spirit that dwelleth in thee. For the Spirit of God that was given unto this flesh endureth not sadness neither constraint. Therefore clothe thyself in cheerfulness, which hath favour with God always, and is acceptable unto Him, and rejoice in it. For every cheerful man worketh good and thinketh good and despiseth sadness ; but the sad man is always committing sin." [1] The same childlike gladness centuries after marked Saint Francis

[1] Hermas, " Mand.," 10, 2, about A.D. 140.

of Assisi and his first disciples, when they went barefoot through the towns of Italy, as the *joculatores Domini,* " the Lord's merry men."

> La lor concordia e i lor lieti sembianti,
> Amore e maraviglia e dolce sguardo,
> Faceano esser cagion di pensier santi.

The same light has shone in the faces of hundreds in our own day, who have found salvation in one or other of the popular evangelistic movements. " I feel like singing all the time," says one of their naïve hymns, and it seems in many cases to say no more than the truth.

Christianity is the religion of sadness. As it looks back over the line of great men who prepared its way in the old Israel, it sees one after another called to a post of lonely antagonism to the world about them, charged with a burden of woe, that they could not but deliver with breaking hearts and passionate tears. Of the Founder of Christianity it is recorded that He wept, but never that He laughed. " Blessed are ye that weep now," " Woe to you that laugh now," are sayings attributed to Him. " I will forewarn you whom ye shall fear : Fear him, which after he hath killed hath power to cast into hell." " I have continual sorrow in my heart," wrote the apostle Paul. " The whole creation groaneth and travaileth in pain together until now," he says in another place. Medieval Christianity made abundance of tears, fasting, and self-affliction typical characteristics of its saints. Protestantism has protested against the type as Popish, but now it is not uncommon to hear Protestantism censured on the very ground that, as compared with Catholicism, it shows a deeper cast of gloom. Especially Protestantism in its more pronounced

A Paradox of Christianity

Evangelical form is charged with a grim hostility to the innocent pleasures of life. Is there any great religious leader, but he has been in some measure a man of sorrows, and acquainted with grief ? One of the writers in the field of religion who has impressed the present generation, the late Father Tyrrell, wrote in his last book : "In deference to the optimistic gospel of progress, Christians are disposed in these days to modulate or silence this strident note of pessimism ; to feel it as something excessive and mistaken, excusable in disorderly and catastrophic periods. But it is vain to deny that this note is as true to the Gospel of Christ as a cheerful belief in the world is discordant from it. . . ." " The incurable tragedy of human life grows deeper as man rises from the hand-to-mouth simplicity of mere animal existence, extends his knowledge and control of experience, and wakes ever more fully to the sense of his insatiable exigencies. The more truly he is man, the more truly he is miserable." [1] Religious men no doubt often denounce as a total mistake the idea that religion is a gloomy thing. But the extent of the popular idea, the fact that the charge has to be rebutted over and over again, points to its having some basis. There is no smoke without fire. There must at any rate be something in the Christian religion to have caused this almost universal association of it with woe.

These are two not unfaithful descriptions of the same object. And, if so, what are we to say of the antinomy which results ? Perhaps it may be said that this paradox in Christianity has always been recognized, and the phrase of the apostle, " sorrowful, yet always rejoicing,"

[1] " Christianity at the Cross-roads," pp. 165, 127.

may be offered us, as all that can be said in the matter. The implication may be that we have here just one of those apparent contradictions with which religious people like to mystify the profane. If so, the unbeliever is likely to shrug his shoulders and go his way. But the religious may sometimes be too ready to make a mystery an excuse for indolence of thought.

As a matter of fact, it seems impossible for any one to be simultaneously happy and unhappy. The field of consciousness, of course, at any moment covers a multifarious variety of things grouped at varying distances, in varying degrees of dimness, about the point upon which attention is fixed. While my attention is occupied with the meaning of a sentence in a book that I am reading, I am also aware, but in a dimmer way, of the sense of the preceding page, and still more remotely, perhaps, of the fact that my chair is uncomfortable and that some one is playing a piano overhead. Now, of all the mass of things present to my consciousness and subconsciousness at any moment, it is certain that some will be pleasant and some the reverse. According as either predominate, my mood as a whole will be happy or unhappy. When we speak of happiness we mean a predominance of the pleasant things. We do not mean that there are no unpleasant things present to consciousness as well. We can, for instance, often be sure by outward physical signs that a person's momentary mood has a happy complexion, even though we know him to be suffering from toothache. He may be suddenly elated by a piece of good news so that the pain is outweighed. We call the man at such a moment happy. If therefore by the phrase " sorrowful, yet always

A Paradox of Christianity

rejoicing " no more is meant than that sorrowful and joyful things are present side by side in the field of consciousness and subconsciousness, we are only saying something which is true of all moods without distinction. If we mean that the sorrowful and joyful things both predominate, we are using a phrase without meaning.

Taken literally, then, the phrase is either a truism or nonsense. What is the fact which it is intended to represent under the form of paradox ? It must be more than that there are alternations of sorrow and joy in the Christian life, for this again would be nothing distinctive. If again the effect of a man's becoming a Christian were that the sorrowful phases became more frequent, there would be no point in describing him as "always rejoicing"; if the joyful phases became more frequent, there would be no point in describing him as distinctively " sorrowful." May not the explanation be that it is not a question of multiplying either kind of mood in relation to the other, but of *redistribution* ? The result of being re-born is to have a number of wholly new things brought into the field of consciousness, some of which provoke the reaction of great joy and some of great pain. The mood of the man is thenceforward determined more or less by these new stimuli, with the consequence that he does not answer in the same way to the old stimuli. He will thus offer a contrast to the natural man just as much by being happy under circumstances which make the natural man miserable, as by being unhappy at events which would leave the unnatural man untouched. It is not that there is necessarily a greater proportion of black or of white in the Christian life, but that the black and white come in new places, and are therefore each conspicuous and surprising. Can we say that the new life in consequence of the redistribution is *happier*? The life of believer and unbeliever alike, one must remember, is measured by the same earthly clocks; there is only a limited amount of time to be distributed, and if the white sections in the Christian's life are not longer as compared with the black ones, than in the life of the natural man, there might seem to be no sense in calling him happier on the whole. An emotion may, of course, be increased, not only in duration, but in intensity. And it may be urged that even if the white spaces in the Christian's life are not more numerous, their white is a purer, more brilliant white than the white in the other life. But then the blacks may also be a deeper black. As a matter of fact, this increase of intensity in the lights and shades is exactly one of the usual effects of vital religion. A life of more or less uniform grey gives place to a life with a richer content of emotions both of a pleasant and of a painful kind. Religion in this, too, shows its affinity with love.

The fact, however, that the lights and shades are respectively intensified, that the volume of emotion is increased, would not, taken by itself, exclude the possibility that the life, as a whole, might become more painful rather than more happy. This is a possibility which the friends of religion are loath to admit. We may agree that they can justify this unwillingness on several grounds. In the first place, the Christian view of the world is one in which, as Father Tyrrell says, the optimism, and not the pessimism, is the ultimate thing. Whatever reckoning be made of evil as it actually confronts the Christian, he must believe that the good in the total result of the process must immensely outweigh it ; some Christians hold that the end of the evil is to be swallowed up without a trace in the good. The very blackness of the shadow is due to the brightness of the sun. It is the ideal of what man is intended to be in the light of the Christian hope that makes his declension to sensuality and triviality terrible and sad. There is nothing sad about the sensuality and thoughtlessness of animals. In his joy, therefore, the Christian has something of essential value, a fraction which bears in itself the likeness of the whole, an instalment of an infinite more of the same kind to come, whereas in what troubles him he experiences only something which belongs to a transient phase of his existence, the discord which the sequel will make good. The joy is the normal, the grief the abnormal, element. All this would lead us to believe that the Christian life should, under ordinary circumstances, not only have higher lights, but be much happier, on the whole. It does not seem to me to follow that it must necessarily in every case be so. The fact that in the conditions of our present life we can attend only to one point at a time, and that the field of reality is unlimited makes our view at any moment a partial one. Evil is part of that reality as it now confronts us. To this evil, in so far as it represents a perversion of the will from the divine ends of man's being, we are the more sensitive the nearer we are to the mind of God. Every one would allow that the attention of the Christian has sometimes to be directed to evil. Those are the black moments which we noted in his life. Since the mood takes its complexion from the point on which attention is momentarily fixed, he cannot, at those moments, be called happy without an abuse of language. So far as the general happiness of his life is impaired by such moments, it is explained that this pain, this learning at close quarters what the negation of the light of God means, this putting forth of the will in the ache of antagonism, is an experience whose value will be seen when the process is complete. But if we once allow that such black moments may take up any part of the Christian life without making it untrue to its ideal, and admit further that the part they should take up is not uniformly measured in all lives, but differs from individual to individual, it seems a possible supposition that in some lives they actually take up moɪe space than the white moments, and do so rightly.

Partly the extent of life coloured black would depend on outside circumstances. If to all men it must bring pain when ideals they really care about are negatived in the lives most closely associated with their own—and the feeling of the Christian is intensified by the character of his ideals—such pain must be constantly renewed, must form almost a continuous element in life, when the division is between close friends, between husband and wife, between mother and son. By ordinary psychological laws, it will tend to be less and less concentrated in sharp moments of distress, to become a dull, habitual sense of restriction, to make the whole life less buoyant, less clear. A uniform radiance under such circumstances would not show that the life had become more Christian, but that it had lost a sensibility which the Christian ought to have. Or again, it has been the vocation of some men to maintain a lifelong fight against evil currents of their times, which for all their efforts they saw only wax stronger. Jeremiah has his place among the figures

A Paradox of Christianity

which the Christian Church regards as typical of the spiritual life. A Stoic would engage in such a conflict and keep his heart whole by never letting it become really concerned in the issues. The sacrifice demanded of the Hebrew prophet and of some of his Christian successors has been greater. He must put his heart into the cause, even if the breaking of his heart be the result. More generally perhaps the extent of the black moments depends upon temperament. Every one would admit that the spiritual forces included in the Christian life act variously upon different temperaments. To desire to make lives uniform by the suppression of individual characteristics would be as great an error as the opposite one of supposing that by saying " temperament " you justify every extravagance. Nor does saying " temperament " imply that a view of the world expressed in a life has no objective validity, is merely a personal oddity. It is temperament which makes one man a mathematician and another an artist, and yet we believe that the numerical relations and the beauty which they respectively perceive are really there. So in the new field of consciousness opened by the Christian life, temperament will incline one man to be sensitive to its lights and another to be sensitive to its shadows, but they may both perceive aspects of things which are real. However closely variations of temperament may be connected with physiological variations in the bodily system, that does not settle the question what value belongs to the different forms of mentality in which they issue. Even therefore when a change of temperament in a single individual depends upon some physical change, it need not necessarily be that his first vision was true and his later one false, or vice versa ; it may be that in consequence of the physical change his attention has been shifted from one part to another of the great field of reality. Take, for instance, a case so striking as that of Father Hecker. In his earlier period as a Catholic preacher, the note of his preaching was a triumphant optimism. He appealed to what was most robust, independent and erect in his fellow-citizens. It was like the call of a trumpet. But there was something missing, certain people felt, something that had been in the old days a constituent of the Christian life, a note that went with abasement, with the sense of sin, with the broken and contrite spirit. Then came the great change, a change no doubt connected with a nervous breakdown. And now the man who had been taxed with having an insufficient sense of sin was overwhelmed and crushed with the horror of it. It filled the whole field of his vision ; he could see nothing but blackness. . . .

Most people probably will be inclined to dismiss the later mood of Father Hecker as a merely morbid delusion, as reflecting no objective reality. But may it not be that if some one has excluded too obstinately some aspect of reality from his purview, it may be a necessary part of the discipline which this particular individual has to undergo during earthly life, that by a natural reaction the excluded aspect should break upon him and in its turn possess him wholly ? In either phase the man may be equally Christian.

Perhaps it is necessary to point out that the line of thought we have followed does not imply that the shadows in the life of a Christian are all things which ought to be there. No Christian is governed entirely by motives belonging to the New Life, and it will in a majority of cases, no doubt, be the working of the old life which clouds and hinders his happiness, and not fidelity to the spiritual vision. In practice a merely sour and ungenial temper may pass itself off as righteous antagonism to evil. All this is perfectly true. The view which condemns all gloom as such, in the Christian life, is likely, if taken as a practical guide, to lead to more right than wrong judgements in particular cases. But it would not be always right ; and sometimes it would be appallingly wrong. There is a necessary element of gloom in the Christian life—or perhaps the term " gloom " is misleading, since it suggests an idle brooding upon evil, and the grief of the Christian ought always to be the nerve of strenuous action, even when the only action possible is prayer.

If these reflections are true, the common well-meant description of the Christian life as the religion of cheerfulness is ill-considered. A defence attempted on such lines must inevitably break down. The charge that Christianity conduces to sorrow must be admitted as, in certain respects, true. The charge, however, need be considered fatal to its claims only on two suppositions ; one, that there is nothing of higher value than cheerfulness ; two, that this life is judged by itself as a final result, not as the part of a much larger whole. It is well to be perfectly frank ; if these suppositions are made, and a scheme of life constructed upon them, that scheme would not be the Christian one. It is no good pretending that Christianity has, as it were, a second string to its bow, so that even if its transcendent hope should be an illusion, it might at any rate be justified as furnishing the sort of life required for this world upon the two suppositions stated. No doubt, Christians in their eagerness to

Hellenism and Christianity

commend their riches are apt to allow the instinct of the salesman to prevail over absolute candour. But the experienced salesman knows that even as a matter of policy it does not pay in the long run to sell upon false pretences. It is a lesser evil that certain individuals should be repelled by the unvarnished statement than that people supposing themselves to acquire a thing of one sort should find that they have got something of quite another sort.

As a matter of fact some three hundred years before the Founder of Christianity was born, another man whom his followers adored for many generations as the Light of mankind had framed a scheme of life deliberately and consistently upon the two suppositions in question. If we are to set out with the principle that cheerfulness is the end of life, and that life means this life only and nothing beyond, then it is hard to see that we can much improve upon the teaching of Epicurus, who carried out the consequences of these principles with the straightforwardness and lucidity of a Greek thinker. It was not in unrestrained indulgence or in vehement passions that Epicurus saw the secret of happiness, but just in the maintenance of a clear and level cheerfulness, an unspoilt appetite for simple pleasures, a freedom from dark and troublous thoughts, especially thoughts connected with religion, with a supposed Something beyond the healthful sunny fields of this life. There is no point upon which the ancient followers of Epicurus pour out their gratitude to their Master more ecstatically than that he had delivered them from religion, from all the terrors of the Beyond. Life might now proceed with the whole of that element clean eliminated for good—

A Paradox of Christianity

not thrust, as it is apt to be in our half-hearted way of
doing things, into some dim, doubtful background,
where it can still make trouble, but disposed of once for
all. Epicurus saw clearly that the great rule dictated by
the principle of cheerfulness was moderation, to confine
desires within a practicable compass, not to take up more
room at the feast of life than is necessary, to enjoy our
share while it lasts, and to rise up cheerful and content
when it is done. He disagreed as much with the volup-
tuary who disturbed the pleasant tenour of life with
violent gratifications as he would have disagreed, had
he known them, with those ardent Hebrew spirits, whose
days were consumed in agonizing for righteousness. Excess
of virtue, no less than excess of vice, is fatal to cheerfulness.
" Be not righteous overmuch, be not overmuch wicked,"
writes a disillusioned Hebrew, who had perhaps tasted
something of the wisdom of the Gentiles.[1] Nor can we
say that Epicurus held up a pattern of merely selfish
happiness for the individual. He knew quite well that
man is a social being, who can only maintain his happiness
on the condition of sharing it. That is why the duties
and delights of friendship had such a prominent position
in his system. If the apparently accidental tie which
bound citizen to citizen was loosened for the Epicurean,
all the stronger was the self-chosen tie which bound him
to his personal friends. This mutual service between
individuals naturally congenial was social service in its
most delightful, immediately rewarding form. It seemed
to secure all the happy element in unselfishness with none
of the disagreeableness involved in service rendered to
the unthankful and evil. It was an unselfishness limited

[1] Ecclesiastes vii, 16.

and reasonable, like everything else which formed a constituent of the cheerful life.

If this scheme of life is really preferable to the Christian one, it would be better frankly to put Epicurus in the place of Christ. Epicurus would be a teacher far safer, saner, and truer than Jesus. One ought not to be misled by the sentiment attaching to the latter Name to allow it more reverence than that of the clear-sighted and fine-tempered Athenian. Least of all ought we to make our practical rule of life Epicurean, and claim to be exponents of the Christian spirit. Epicureanism stands on quite another basis, with a clear, consistent, workable scheme of its own. Workable, of course, up to a certain point, under certain conditions. In its modern forms, no less than in its ancient, the philosophy of cheerfulness seems to demand a certain level of physical well-being. The persons whom we hear profess it, enjoy a fair measure of health, of comfort, of prosperity. We cannot guarantee it against the more shattering blows of fortune, the more hideous accidents. And the worst of it is that shattering blows and hideous accidents may happen any day to any of us. Now security was felt by the ancient Greeks far more keenly than by ourselves to be a *sine qua non* of happiness. Epicurus knew that it would be no use to present his countrymen with any scheme of life which would not guarantee them against every possible mischance. The " wise " man, the man who had got the secret of life, must be able to be happy in the red-hot bull of Phalaris, because, after all, the bull of Phalaris was a possible contingency and a scheme of life which failed to provide for it was like a leaky vessel. And yet it was certain that the cloudy thing we call To-morrow

A Paradox of Christianity

was beyond man's reach, to discover or subjugate or secure. And if man's happiness lay in its hand, where was he ? Epicurus had to face the difficulty, and he did so in a curious way. The Future with its unexplored possibilities lay beyond man's control ; yes, but there was something of which he had firm possession, which could never be taken from him, upon which under all circumstances his happiness could be stablished unshaken —the Past. He need be troubled by no looking forward, if his memories offered him an unassailable refuge. If the Future changed into a hideous Present, in a moment he could be away from it all, back among the delightful hours of long ago, the beautiful things he had loved, summer days under the plane-trees, old laughter, hours when the heart had glowed with new vision, friend sitting hand in hand with friend. The true Epicurean, the Master said, could be happy in the bull of Phalaris.

There is a splendid boldness about this attempt to fortify the weak place of the system, yet one cannot call it successful. It is in conflict with a plain truth of psychology, that the Future is to us of far greater concern than the Past. It is not equally distressing to expect a violent pain to-morrow and to remember one yesterday. Probably the poet was nearer to the facts of human nature who said that there was

> Nessun maggior dolore
> Che ricordarsi del tempo felice
> Nella miseria.

The escape offered by Epicurus was futile. And yet one must always remember with what heroism he himself held to his theory when it was put to the test of practice. We have part of the letter he wrote to one of his friends

Hellenism and Christianity

a little before his death. " The day on which I write this brings my life to a close, and I reckon it happy. Incessant is the torment in bladder and bowels, so great as to exhaust all possibilities of pain, but all these things are outmatched by the joy in the soul, when I call to mind our conversations of old. And do thou act worthily of the disposition thou hast had from a boy towards me and towards philosophy, by taking care of the children of Metrodorus." It was, however, in reality a triumph, not for the system of Epicurus, but for his own greatness of spirit.

A joy that can prevail over severe bodily pain is also offered by Christ. It has been possessed by martyrs in as fierce ordeals as the bull of Phalaris, even by persons who do not seem to have much natural heroism—frail women and children. And Christianity may appear so far to make the same sort of promise as the philosophy of cheerfulness, leaving it only to be decided which can fulfil the promise best. But it is not so. With its joy Christianity introduces new pains. It gives no guarantee of uniform, or even of predominant, cheerfulness. It is therefore not a question which system fulfils a promise best, but which makes the best promise. It is a question whether the two suppositions upon which the philosophy of cheerfulness is based are right.

The first supposition is that cheerfulness is the thing most worth having. And here we have to take note of the remarkable fact that this has been denied by many thinkers, who stand quite apart from the Christian hope. " The highest sort of happiness," George Eliot said, " often brings so much pain with it, that we can only tell it from pain by its being what we would choose before

A Paradox of Christianity

everything else, because our souls see it is good." [1]
Indeed, why should one try to tell it from pain ? It *is*
pain ; and yet we see that it is good. It may seem
strange that when cheerfulness is such an obviously good
and desirable thing, the attempt to make it the best thing
should be repudiated by many spirits with an emotion
amounting to disgust and indignation. They feel that
there are kinds of sorrow in which man realizes a worth,
a greatness, which is impossible on the level of cheerfulness. Without these elements of sorrow, life would be
altogether a smaller affair, something that was less worth
serious concern, something to be taken more lightly. And
while they can endure to see life tragic, they cannot endure
to see it trivial. Now, if persons of this temper were an
isolated species, one might regard them as suffering
from a regrettable megalomania. But it seems that they
only give voice to an instinct wide as humanity. Why
is it that tragedy should necessarily be felt to have a
greater dignity than comedy ? What is it that makes
us seek spectacles, poems, romances which touch the
spring of tears, except that in the emotion we have a
sense of growing greater, of winning heights ? Why is
it that such a word as " serious " is used both to express
greater fulness of reality and something akin to sadness ?
What profound feeling is it that would be outraged by
a perfectly harmless comic picture if we saw it set above
an altar, that *is* outraged by a *Vie de Jesus-Christ pour
rire* ? It is as if we could allow the comic, the laughter-
making, only in the subordinate places of life, like the
grotesque figures which the medieval builders set upon
pillars and cornices in their churches, but never in the

[1] " Romola," Epilogue.

173

Hellenism and Christianity

principal places, where the worshipper had converse with the highest things. Sorrow, on the other hand, has the freedom of the whole sanctuary, and in the holiest place is an emblem of pain. Yes, even in that ancient world, where it arose, the philosophy of Epicurus—so comely, so sensible, so genial—came into conflict with some deep instinct which repudiated it as taking from man his peculiar dignity. " A swine of Epicurus' herd " became proverbial. His doctrine was misconstrued by unworthy disciples, it is said. True ; but was not this in part just because it lacked in its appeal something which kept men on a high level, that there was a secret ignobility in its essence which the unworthy disciples made patent ? It was not sour Northern Puritans, it was all that was best in that lively Greek and Roman world which flung Epicureanism from it and rallied to the austere call of Stoicism.

Christianity holds that this instinct man has of his greatness really corresponds with his destinies. It therefore denies the second supposition which underlies the philosophy of cheerfulness, the supposition which limits our view to this world. If each human life is really only a momentary phenomenon and ceases absolutely at death, then man really is a much smaller thing than he had supposed, and nothing in human life really does matter very much. Life really is comparatively trivial, and it is ridiculous to make such a fuss about it. The instinct of which we spoke must then be pronounced a kind of universal megalomania after all. Unfortunately, even if it proved to be such, it subsists as a fact, and to those who have it at all strongly, the discovery of the real triviality of life would be intolerable. They would

A Paradox of Christianity

wish to be rid of it at once. " Fortune may bring upon me all her tragic storms, but play a part in this sordid farce—that she shall never make me do ! If this life is all, I end it here." On the other hand, if the Christian view is true, if upon this life hang eternal issues for the eternal spirit, then man's sense of his greatness and of the high seriousness of life is in accordance with reality. The individual life in this world would then have to be judged simply as the part of a vaster whole, and it is obvious that what is goodness in a part need not be goodness in a whole—the discord, for instance, made good by the sequel ? It is therefore open to Christians to admit that their scheme of life is a bad one, if this life only is considered, and yet believe it good from the standpoint of eternity. Indeed, Christianity finds a truth in the philosophy of cheerfulness no less than in the philosophy of sadness. While it believes that man cannot be great in this phase of his existence without a measure of sadness, it believes that the ideal aimed at by the philosophy of cheerfulness is more like what the aspect of man's exist-ence, looked at as a whole, would be. Only that philosophy wishes, as it were, to compress the effect of the whole tune within the single bar, and makes every-thing cramped and mean in consequence. Its cheerfulness is a poor imitation of the joy in which the whole pain of the spiritual life is taken up in its breadth and intensity, and transcended. But for such transcending the Christian knows that the scale of eternity is needed, and that apart from that scale his scheme for this life cannot be justified.

There is no denying it. Christianity makes men set their all upon an " if." Against this human prudence naturally protests. Those who spoil this life, relying upon one beyond, lose, if there *is* nothing beyond, their one opportunity. This life at any rate is something substantial, and if they make a success of it, then, even if there be no other, they will have got something ; as Christians, they run the risk of getting nothing at all. They would prefer to find a scheme of life which would secure them in both alternatives, yield a predominant measure of contentment, as far as this life is concerned, and at the same time conduct them on the right way towards another, if another there be. And they hear so much about the happiness possessed by Christians even in this life, that Christianity might seem at first just to meet their requirements. But let them not deceive themselves ! Christianity will lead them a little along the way they wish to go, and then betray them. It will give them a spell of joy, and then suddenly bring them into strange distresses. The philosophy of cheerfulness is the philosophy of moderation, of the golden mean ; and Christianity runs to extremes. It is violent, being a kind of Love, and not even the inmost recesses of the soul are safe from its stormy invasion. It may often wear a smiling face ; but admit it, and it will work wreckful havoc in a man's life. Its word that a man embracing it must be prepared to lose his life will be found to be dread earnest ; he must fling literally all upon the venture.

We, to whom hedging is so congenial, find ourselves confronted with an inexorable necessity of choice. Christ is resolute, that a man choosing Him should make a real leap—no clinging to solid earth—a real leap into immensity. That has been so always. An old Christian writer, rehearsing the traditional types of spiritual greatness,

A Paradox of Christianity

finds that the characteristic of all was "faith," and that "faith" was just this abandonment of near and certain and palpable goods for the sake of a good invisible, hypothetical—Abraham leaving his country to become a wanderer, Moses leaving the splendour of Pharaoh's house to become an outcast, and so on with the rest. They all elected to give up this life. "They were stoned, they were sawn asunder, they were tempted, they were slain with the sword : they went about in sheepskins, in goatskins ; being destitute, afflicted, evil entreated, wandering in deserts and mountains and caves, and the holes of the earth." And all for a "promise" which they never received ! [1]

There is thus no concealment on the part of Christianity of its whole scheme standing or falling by a hypothesis. Supposing the promised sequel fails, it has made life a discord, and it leaves it at that. As a discord, it must be pronounced simply a failure. Not that Christianity concerns itself with the other life to the exclusion of this, or means simply that a Christian "goes to heaven when he dies," but it concerns itself with this life as a phase in an eternal process. It spoils life from the point of view of those who take it as the complete and final expression of an ideal. It spoils life —who has not known striking examples ? The spoiling does not perhaps appear in cases where a man's pre-Christian life was one of pronounced vice, or misery, for excess on that side, as Epicurus taught, disturbs the happy balance no less than excess on the other, and the vicious or miserable life will probably appear spoilt already. But where the pre-Christian life was simply

[1] Hebrews xi, 37-39.

Hellenism and Christianity

Epicurean—bent in its moderate way on securing a reasonable amount of enjoyment tempered by a reasonable amount of unselfishness in the service of friends, no account being taken of any hypothetical Beyond—then we may see how the general content and smoothness of such an existence is confounded by the working of the new motives! The man who before was walking gracefully and well along the level begins to climb, and we have a sorry spectacle of false steps and slidings back, and awkward postures. There is no denying that as a performance the walking was more successful and pleasant to watch; there is no denying that if he could climb without false steps and slidings back it would be better; there is no denying that if there is nothing up there to climb for, he had much better never have tried to climb at all.

We cannot prove that man's belief in his own greatness is not megalomania; we cannot prove that life is really momentous and not trivial. Whenever we elect one hypothesis rather than another on the ground of *nobleness*—as, for instance, when we elect to trust a friend in spite of appearances—there is an element of voluntary determination in our choice. And when men deliberately decide to sacrifice this life for the sake of a larger Whole, apprehended only by faith, their choice is something of this kind, and they take the risks of being deceived open-eyed. At any rate, any individual who does so makes his choice in a company of which he need not be ashamed, the "great cloud of witnesses," and he looks to One Figure who shows the way, the Initiator of his faith. To Him the vast significance of life was measured by the depth of His pain. It was a reality which was worth

A Paradox of Christianity

all that ; as large and profound as that was to be the ultimate joy. Renan, with the quick play of his fancy, asks a question which to many people has seemed simply profane. To some perhaps it will be singularly fruitful of suggestion. He asks whether the thought may not have come to Jesus in Gethsemane that after all He would have done better to settle down in Nazareth, as the husband of Mary, the sister of Martha, to an ordinary, quiet, humanly happy life ? Instead of being shocked, it might be well to face the question : Why not ? If the philosophy of cheerfulness is right, why not ? What is really the point or purpose or reason in all this agony ? Does it not imply a hugely exaggerated estimate of the importance of life ? And behind the one bowed Figure of Jesus we may see the long lines of other agonizers for the Ideal, the immeasurable volume of pain, not caused by any bodily hurt or accidental ill, but taken by men upon themselves voluntarily, taken into their hearts, because the souls of men seemed to them worth all that. The philosophy of cheerfulness and common sense must pronounce against them all—megalomania.

X

HUMAN PROGRESS

IT has been often remarked that of our most fundamental beliefs we are likely to have no articulate
consciousness. There are things we take so much
for granted that it has never occurred to us to affirm
them as truths. One belief which I think forms part
of the persistent background of the world-view prevalent
among us here in the West—and prevalent probably
wherever our modern Western civilization has had influence—is the belief that the movement of the world into
which we have been born is a movement in a definite
direction, a movement from worse to better, or lower
to higher, in some sense at any rate in its main trend
a *forward* movement. We see plenty of evil round us
still uncured ; there are abuses and injustice of all sorts
against which the young man is prepared to wage battle,
but if any prophet assured him that a hundred years
hence those abuses and that injustice would be exactly
where they are to-day, that the attack upon them would
have failed to achieve any improvement at all, he would
find it almost impossible to believe. Just as when we
are being driven in a carriage up a mountain, while we
may be thinking and talking of other things there is always
there present in the background of our consciousness

the sense of upward movement, so the sense of upward movement is always with us to-day, giving tone to our thoughts and discussions upon all the questions of the hour.

Now, what ground have we for believing that progress is a permanent characteristic of human history, that it will go on in the future ?

Belief in progress has by no means been a universal characteristic of human thought. It seems to me to belong essentially to that form of civilization which has been developed during the last few centuries in Europe.

Among the ancient Greeks, so far from the sense of upward movement just described having been general, one gathers that a sense of downward movement prevailed. There was, of course, no one generally accepted dogmatic system, but a mass of floating popular ideas, and in later classical times a variety of dogmatic teachings framed in the different philosophical schools. When we turn to popular belief, we discover a general conviction that the Golden Age lay in the past, and that the present was an age of degeneracy and decline. In Homer there is no definite allusion to a Golden Age, but in describing the feats of the heroes he will glance at his own day to complain that men are not now what they once were ; this is a punier breed ; Diomedes " caught up in his hand a stone, a great mass, which two men could not carry, such as men are now. But the son of Tydeus swung it easily by himself." In another old poet, Hesiod, we get the theory of the successive ages of mankind set forth at length, which remained always a piece of current mythology. " Golden was the race of men which at the first the immortal gods made, who dwell on high. These were they who lived in the days of Kronos, when he ruled in heaven; and they lived like gods, with a spirit free from care, apart from all labours and misery. There was no wretched old age to follow, but with hands and feet always as in youth they took delight in good cheer out of all reach of evils. When they died, it was like men overborne by sleep. All good things were theirs. The corn-giving soil rendered fruit of itself, much and without stint, and they wrought as they would their works in easefulness with abundance of good things." Then followed the Silver Age, markedly inferior to the first, and the Bronze Age, still more degenerate, and again after the heroic age which the poet is obliged to intercalate in this point to make his ages square with other parts of popular mythology, comes last the Iron Age, in which the poet laments that his lot has fallen. The world is full of evil, all the social relations will be perverted; the old kindness of host and guest, brother and brother will go; children will dishonour their parents. There will be no reverence for the gods; no respect for the upright and true man, but honour rather for the evil-doer and violent. "And then the two goddesses, Shamefastness and Right Indignation, covering their fair faces with their white robes, will depart to heaven from the wide earth, to go to the race of the Immortals and leave men behind them. And for mortal men nothing but grief and pain will be left; and evil there will be no way to withstand."

In some form or other this idea, that the present is vastly inferior to an ideal past, seems to have been general in classical antiquity. In the philosophic schools naturally an attempt was made to get a more far-reaching

view of the universe, and here the notion was elaborated
of the process of things being a cyclic movement in which
history repeated itself over and over again without any
end.   It was the Stoic school, the school of widest popular
influence in the later times of antiquity, which gave this
theory its most elaborate form.   Every world period,
according to the Stoics, ended in a conflagration when
all the separate elements of the world were unified once
more in the Primal Fire, and then from the Primal Fire
the process began again, and so on for ever.   And the
correspondence between one epoch and another, they
taught, was exact point for point.   All the details of our
individual lives would be repeated to infinity.   Over and
over again Socrates would marry Xanthippe and drink
the hemlock and die.   And looking at the history of
mankind within each of these world periods, the Stoics,
like the people generally, saw it as a process of decline.
There was an advance in one sense, in the arts and crafts
and the complexity of life.   As compared with the primitive age, their own age had grown in scientific knowledge,
in all the devices of material civilization ; it could navigate
the seas and fill its houses with the good things of remote
lands ; but with this advance there had gone continuous
moral decline.   It was in the age of primitive simplicity
that men had lived in harmony with nature, virtuous
and happy.   Decline within each period, and the periods
endlessly repeating themselves in an unvarying round
—this yielded a very different view of the world from
our buoyant assurance that things are moving onward
to something wonderful and new.   Contemplation of such
a world could only lead men to turn away from it as
utterly flat and stale.

Hellenism and Christianity

An unknown Jewish writer of the Greek age, apparently influenced by the tone of the Gentile world around him, has put the exposition of such a view into the mouth of one of the ancient kings of his people. " Vanity of vanities, saith the Preacher ; vanity of vanities, all is vanity. What profit hath man of all his labour wherein he laboureth under the sun ? . . . All things are full of weariness ; man cannot utter it ; the eye is not satisfied with seeing, nor the ear with hearing. That which hath been is that which shall be ; and that which hath been done is that which shall be done ; and there is no new thing under the sun. Is there a thing whereof men say, See this is new ? It hath been already in the ages which were before us. . . . I have seen all the works that are done under the sun ; and behold all is vanity and a striving after wind."

Some three hundred years after this was written, the authentic testimony of a sage seated upon a throne was given to posterity. The Emperor Marcus Aurelius, steeped in the philosophy of his Greek masters, overlooked a realm far wider than Solomon's. Plato had once said that the world would be reformed when philosophers became kings. And into the hands of this philosopher was now put the whole of the Greco-Roman world. It was the time when the Roman system of imperial govern-ment was at its greatest perfection, when, in Gibbon's view, the " fairest part of the earth and the most civilized portion of mankind " enjoyed extraordinary prosperity and happiness. But the sad eye of its ruler kindled with no interest as he looked at the huge fabric of his empire and its historic glories ; his beautiful and ascetic figure seems to stand out upon a background of monotonous dullness; it is with a great weariness of spirit, without any spring or any hope, that we see him addressing himself to his imperial duty. " It is Nature's work to shift and to transpose, to remove thence and carry thither. All is change; yet need we not fear any novelty; all is the wonted round; nay, even the apportionments equal. . . . All comes to stench and refuse at last. . . . All things are alike—familiar, fleeting, foul: everything as it was in the days of the dead and buried. . . . Anon earth will cover us all; then earth in its turn will change; then the resultant of the change; then the resultant of the resultant, and so *ad infinitum*. The billows of change and variation roll apace, and he who ponders them will feel contempt for all things mortal. . . . Endeavour the best you may; do not hope for Utopia. . . . How silly and how strange to think anything in life wonderful! . . . He who sees what now is, hath seen all, all that was from eternity, all that shall be without end; for all things are of one kind and of one form. . . . As in the amphitheatre, or other places of amusement, the monotony of tedious repetitions makes the spectacle pall, so is it with the experience of life; up and down, everything is one monotonous round. How long? how long? . . . As from some eminence survey the countless herds of men—their thronging festivals, their voyages of storm and voyages of calm, the chequered phases of their appearance, action, disappearance; or imagine again the life of ages past, the life of generations to come, the life now living among savage tribes; how many have never heard your name, how many will at once forget it! How many who perhaps applaud you now, will very soon revile! How valueless in sooth is memory, or fame, or all else put together!" Marcus Aurelius has no hope for the world; only a message for the individual, bidding him seek his good within himself.

When we turn from the ancient Mediterranean world to India, the similarity of view is striking. Here, too, we find the four ages, beginning with the best and ending with the worst, which, as we saw, belonged to popular Greek mythology; here, too, we find the doctrine of eternal recurrence, which was familiar to the Greek philosophical schools. In India, however, the two views are combined in a single system, which was not the case in Greece. It is the series of four *yugas* which endlessly repeats itself. And while the underlying principle is the same, India has gone much further than Greece in dogmatic systemization. It has not been content with the simple repetition of a *mahāyuga*, but has combined the *mahajugas* in still larger and larger cycles, till we get the elaborate system of orthodox Hinduism and the still more complicated systems of the Jains and Buddhists. But in all cases the effect upon the spirit is the same— to present us with a circular movement, not a progressive one. There is no one " divine event to which the whole creation moves." Even if, whenever there is lack of righteousness and wrong arises, the Divine Being again enters the sphere of humanity " for the protection of the good, for the destruction of the wicked, and for the sake of establishing righteousness," no such reforms can mean any final salvation for the world, which is bound upon the eternal wheel. There *is* no salvation for the world, but only for the individual who turns away from it and seeks salvation within himself.

This was the conclusion to which thinkers had come

Human Progress

in the ancient classical world of Europe and in ancient India alike, but between them, in Nearer Asia, lay the seats of two peoples whose view contrasted strangely with theirs. These two peoples were the Iranians and the Hebrews. According to the Zoroastrian faith which had come to prevail in Irân some centuries before our era, the course of the world was not circular, but a single process, during which the Good Power and the Evil Power were in conflict, to be ended by the final and complete victory of the Good. The Zoroastrian looked forward to the appearance of a Saviour (*Saoshyant*) in the fullness of time by whose agency evil would be destroyed and all good men brought into a state of everlasting bliss. Such a hope made him see the actual world process in a very different light. Real issues were being fought out, and action was abundantly worth while. Each good Zoroastrian could be a fellow-worker with God, in his own measure a saviour (*saoshyant*), a *frashôcerator*, a " renewer " of humanity and the world.

The other people who looked forward were the Hebrews. In the great prophets who proclaimed to their people the word of its God during the later times of the Israelite kingdoms and the days of exile in Babylonia we have the supreme representatives of the old Hebrew religion. It would indeed be mistaken to seek in their writings any distinct cosmology ; they were not speculators and reasoners, but men who felt profoundly, whose form of expression was poetical rather than philosophic. Their thoughts did not plunge into infinite time, but lit up the needs and the significance of the present. So far as they were predicters, they thought of the future which was even now at the doors, and that future they uniformly

Hellenism and Christianity

represent in dark colours. Their message was primarily one of judgement; the people had become so insensible to its God's requirements of mercy, justice, and truth, that His holiness must be vindicated, not in the glorification of His people, but in its chastisement. And so it must be given into the hand of those peoples who were the instruments of the God of Israel, although they knew not His Name, although they seemed only to obey their own fierce lusts for trampling down and spoiling the earth. But yet the prophets felt that the precious thing committed to Israel could not perish in the overflowing tide of judgement. The one people to whom Yahweh had revealed Himself in a special way could not be blotted out. Beyond the days of darkness and distress and heathen domination they had a vision of wonderful days when their God would show His power in the earth, when there would be a new Israel true to its vocation, ruled by righteous kings, walking in the light of the Lord, blessed among the peoples and a blessing. These visions of judgement and of blessing to follow do not, as we have said, yield any cut-and-dried cosmology; they are clothed in poetical imagery, described in vivid metaphors and similes, in idealized pictures whose elements are taken from the actual world the visionaries knew. But as in the Zoroastrian religion, so here, the world is the stage of a drama in which God Himself mingles to carry His purpose to a worthy consummation. It is worth while being interested in it; it is worth while, when the Lord's voice is heard asking, "Whom shall I send and who will go for us?" to answer instantly, "Here am I; send me."

These two peoples, the Persian and the Hebrew, came

by the development of events into a close relation, as ruler and ruled. And to this connexion some modifications which the Hebrew body of ideas underwent in later phases can probably be traced. Instead of the vague poetical conceptions of the old prophets, bearing closely on the present and the immediate future, we get the world-view of the apocalyptic writings, the series of which is opened by the book of Daniel. Hebrew speculation now, like Zoroastrian, ranges over the whole scheme of human history and sets about marking off and measuring the successive epochs ; poetry gives place to dogmatic precision. But although the form is changed, the underlying conviction that the present is very evil, that a Divine judgement is imminent, and that the judgement is to usher in a final consummation of blessedness for the righteous, this remains the same. The apocalyptic writers no doubt had a more transcendent phantasmagoric conception of the judgement and the future kingdom than Isaiah and Jeremiah ; the important thing is that the face of the Hebrew in both cases was turned forwards and illuminated with the glory of a day to come, a crowning appearance in power of the God of righteousness.

This hope passed over from Judaism to the Christian Church, though now, of course, it had a new personal thrill, in so far as the glorified Figure which was to form the centre of the stupendous future was no longer a merely ideal conception, but the Master who had been intimately known here in the common world of men. At any moment in the thought of the early Christian the whole order of things round about him might be brought to an abrupt end, and the Son of Man appear upon the clouds of heaven. Then, as time went on, and the generation which had seen the Lord lay far behind, the consummation was looked for at some remoter future. The hope receded, it no longer filled the whole of life and made the things of the actual world of no account. But although the end lay further off, it was still the goal to which the whole course of human history tended. Christianity, like Zoroastrianism and like Judaism, has turned men's faces forwards, and made this drama of human history no mere revolution of the wheel, but a process of unique significance and value.

One ought also to note that the Christian hope has passed strangely unaltered into the system of Islam. In the Mohammedan view also the course of history is a unique process leading to a single consummation ; but it is remarkable that Islam should have continued to make the Person of Jesus Christ the central Figure in the last scene of the human drama, that it should look still for His Second Coming, His and none other's, to usher in the end.

From considering these different views which have prevailed among men in Europe and Asia, we return to our own time and ask what is the meaning of this general assurance that the human race is making progress. The assurance seems to me to rest on two bases, a scientific base and a religious base. Let us first take the scientific.

To some large extent the assurance of progress seems to be a product of the theory of Evolution which has become popular since Darwin. This theory seems exactly the reverse of the ancient view which saw human history as a series of lapses from an ideal primitive state of virtue and happiness. The further back we go, according to the Darwinian view, the more man approximates to

Human Progress

the beast. Instead of the gracious half-divine figures of the Golden Age, of the *krtayuga*, we are shown a breed of hairy gorilla-like creatures, huddling and jibbering in caves and tearing each other in the blind struggle for life. Instead of the primeval sages, sources of an immemorial wisdom, whose antiquity is its very title to reverence, we are shown magicians and medicine-men overawing savage tribes with practices of crude superstition ; for a primitive revelation of Divine truth we get a jumble of totems and fetishes and taboos. From the beast to primitive man, from primitive man to the man of to-day, the human race has achieved its painful ascent, and if all this time the road has been upward, is it not natural to think that the goal must lie somewhere yet further up, out of sight, that any descent of the road we may seem to mark at this point or that must be only a local anomaly to be compensated for by new elevations further on ? This view, which became general among educated people in the days of Victoria, has been given its consecration in poetry by the great voice of the age.

Red of the dawn !
Is it turning a fainter red ? so be it, but when shall we lay
    The Ghost of the Brute that is walking and haunting us yet,
       and be free ?
    In a hundred, a thousand winters ? Ah, what will *our* children be,
The men of a hundred thousand, a million summers away ?
    *   *   *   *   *
Where is one that, born of woman, altogether can escape
From the lower world within him, moods of tiger, or of ape ?
    Man as yet is being made, and ere the crowning Age of ages,
Shall not æon after æon pass and touch him into shape ?

All about him shadow still, but, while the races flower and fade,
Prophet-eyes may catch a glory slowly gaining on the shade,
    Till the peoples all are one, and all their voices blend in choric
Hallelujah to the Maker, " It is finished. Man is made."

Hellenism and Christianity

These passages of Tennyson show us admirably, I think, the two bases upon which the current optimistic view of human progress rests. The influence of the Darwinian theory is obvious, but it is supplemented by the conviction that human history is controlled by a Divine purpose: "Hallelujah to the Maker." But these two fundamental presuppositions are separable. There are a number of men of science who would reject the idea of a Divine Purpose; and one may believe in a Divine Purpose without accepting the Darwinian hypothesis. Can either presupposition taken by itself warrant our belief in progress? The scientific view sets out to determine just what the facts of the world are, as they are discoverable by our five senses, and to inquire what general conclusion can be drawn from the facts so determined. The first question, then, for science is as to plain matter of fact: Has there or has there not been progress on the whole hitherto? Now, if you accept any modern theory of evolution, you must hold that the movement of the world has gone, from the days when life first appeared upon the globe, along a definite line of advance. The types which preceded modern man along the line of descent form, not only a chronological series, but a series of modifications with a uniform tendency, marked by the distance of man from the beast. But when you call this tendency *progress*, you imply that there is an increase of good along the line, a change from lower to higher in some scale of spiritual *value*, and this at once raises questions as to our *standards* of good, of value. Undoubtedly man is a much more complex being than the beasts, undoubtedly modern man is a much more complex being than primitive man. He has developed a much wider and subtler range of sensibilities and interests. There can be no question either about the expansion of his logical intelligence ; he knows a great deal more in the conscious intellectual way about the world and about himself. Through his knowledge his command over the forces of nature has enormously increased ; he can provide for his material comfort to-day to an extent unparalleled in any earlier age. All these things, however, may be admitted, and it may still be asked whether these developments have led from a better to a worse ? is it *better* to be a modern man than a primitive cave-dweller ? And this is not a speculative question merely. It is one urgently practical, because our own individual efforts can in their measure help on or retard this process, and before flinging ourselves into this struggle, we surely want to know whether there is any worthy end to be secured ; whether it is worth while sacrificing ourselves in order to further what is called *progress*.

Now, when we come to questions of ultimate value argument is difficult ; each individual is thrown back upon his own inner convictions. But if the convictions of the individual agree with a large consensus, there is so far ground for believing them to be true. There is certainly a large consensus that this development of mankind has been from lower to higher, that the more complex type is the superior type. This is implied in all popular language ; people generally have no doubt that one man is of more value than many sparrows, that the civilized man is on a higher level than the savage. And this view I personally believe to be true. I think, however, that in stating it we must guard against misconceptions. We can judge value, I suppose, both by a scale of happiness and a scale of moral goodness. But if we put the question simply in the form, Is civilized man happier than savage man ? is civilized man better morally than savage man ? this would, it seems to me, be misleading. As a matter of fact it seems questionable whether in mere volume and intensity of pleasure the savage hunter has not as much as the civilized man gets from a sonata of Beethoven's or a play of Shakespeare's. Or, again, whether in volume and intensity the devotion which leads the primitive man to sacrifice himself for his tribe, or the primitive mother to sacrifice herself for her child, is not as great as the loyalty which leads a civilized man to sacrifice himself for the good of humanity, or for some spiritual ideal. What makes the civilized happiness more worth having is not that it is greater in bulk, but that because the civilized man is more complex, with subtler sensibilities, his happiness is very much richer in content. What makes his morality more worth having is not that it implies an intenser loyalty, but a much more extensive one, that it covers a wider field, that the sphere of duties has been extended beyond the tribe to the nation, and beyond the nation to mankind.

But now comes the further question. Supposing it is true that hitherto mankind has made progress, can Science give us any guarantee that this progress will go on indefinitely ? And to this question, I gather, the only answer can be No Natural science, taken by itself, holds out no hope of the perpetual progress of the human race. If evolution has worked out so far in an advance of man from lower to higher, from worse to

better, this has been merely an accidental effect. There
is nothing in the law of evolution itself to make change
an improvement. That law, in the Darwinian acceptance,
is the working of blind chance ; it says only that the
type most adapted to its environment will be the most
likely to survive ; it says nothing about the quality of
the type judged in the scale of spiritual value. Nor
does scientific theory usually stop at declaring the continued progress of the human race merely doubtful. It
draws a definite line somewhere in the future at which
the history of mankind must come to a stop. According
to the general agreement of scientific men, the days of
the earth are numbered. And in the last stages of the
life of mankind the evils of the physical environment,
whether increasing cold or increasing heat or drought,
will more and more prevail over any efforts the doomed
race can make to meet them. There must come a time
when humanity reaches the summit of its ascent, and,
however long it may continue upon that high level, sooner
or later the descent must begin, the days of continuous
defeat by the great blind forces of Nature. And who
can say but that we have come to the summit now, that
the world will never be any better than it is to-day, and
in process of time will begin to grow worse ?

This is a very different picture from that we read just
now in Tennyson's exalting stanzas. How comes it
that when he has adopted so much of the current scientific theory, he has made so jubilant a forecast ? To
account for this we have to look, I think, at the other
base of our current optimism, the religious. The
general attitude of men had been determined by the
Christian hope, had been made a forward-looking attitude,

Hellenism and Christianity

an expectation of a Divine event which should give meaning to the movement of creation. Tennyson, of course, himself was an independent thinker whose adhesion to Christian belief was deliberate and personal, but the vague notions current among the unreflecting masses of men were themselves largely an outcome of the inherited Christian attitude, even in the case of those who had lost all definite Christian belief. In this way it appears to me that religion is responsible for a great deal of the popular optimism, however little religious colour it may in some quarters display. This brings us to the question, Does the Christian hope, or, to make the inquiry wider, does belief in God, warrant a belief in the continuous progress of humanity on this planet?

And here I think we ought to remark that in some respects the expectation of Tennyson, the expectation of ordinary educated men, has become different from the primitive Christian view. Both look forward in hope to a Divine event, but whereas with the primitive Christian that event was thought of as catastrophic and close at hand, a sudden shattering of the existent order by the manifestation of the Divine power, with the modern man it is a *far-off* Divine event led up to by a gradual process of evolution. From the modern man's point of view the primitive Christian view was based upon a perfectly true spiritual conviction that the history of mankind must terminate in a Divine consummation, but this conviction was clothed in dramatic imagery which had symbolic, and not literal, truth. He feels therefore at liberty to adopt from Science the idea of a gradual evolution and retain the Christian hope so far as it envisages a worthy end. I am not sure that this combination is legitimate.

Human Progress

Science, taken by itself, does not point to any continuous progress; the original Christian hope, taken by itself, does not point to any progress at all, because the Divine intervention was expected to be abrupt and transcendent. How, then, by *combining* two such views can we get warrant for the belief in a process of gradual amelioration and a Divine event which is the outcome of that process?

Christianity certainly implies a belief that the world process is one of unique significance, governed by a Divine Purpose, and subordinated to a worthy end. This is essential to the Christian assurance, and indeed to all forms of genuine Theism. But I do not feel that the Christian faith *necessitates* a belief in the progress of humanity upon this planet, in the improvement of the world. If one may incline to this view as a reasonable hope, we cannot have the same assurance about it, as we can have about there being a Divine Purpose—that there is somewhere or somehow a worthy end which will make all the travail of humanity worth while. This conviction may stand like a rock, but that the worthy end will take the form of a gradual amelioration on this planet is, I think, less certain.

We cannot surely deny that a man may hold another view on this point without being untrue to the fundamental Christian assurance. Such another view was recently urged with great pathos and eloquence by a Christian thinker, the late George Tyrrell, in his posthumous book, " Christianity at the Cross-Roads." Tyrrell accepted to the full the view of those scientists who despaired of the future of humanity, as a species inhabiting this globe. He believed, too, that the ills of the world were incurable, that the race would dwindle and perish in a limited number

Hellenism and Christianity

of years. The end which made the process worth while lay, according to him, not in the world of sense at all, but in another plane of being. And he maintained that this view was far more consonant than the current one with the original Christian belief. Like that, it did not contemplate any improvement in the present state of things, but an abrupt passage from this state of things to a transcendent world ; only whereas in the primitive view this abrupt passage was a cosmic event in the near future, in Tyrrell's view it was accomplished individually at death. The march of humanity was upwards, but not along the road of earthly history : the earth was a mere platform which humanity crossed in its journey into the Unseen : man's future lay there, and it did not really matter what happened to the platform. All efforts at social reform, at improving the condition of things here were therefore doomed, according to Tyrrell, to certain failure in the long run. Any temporary success would be outweighed by fresh breakdowns. He denied, however, that this made it futile to engage in the struggle. The transcendental destiny of humanity saved the motive to strive. The struggle had an educational value in this phase of being quite apart from its success.

This view is not one which commends itself to me, but I think it is worthy of serious consideration. I think the current optimism is largely so unreflecting and easy-going, that it was well it should be challenged. Tyrrell's position is one which, so far as I can see, perfectly preserves the essential part of the Christian or the Theistic hope. I feel that if it were proved to me that all attempt to make the world better must fail, I might still be a Christian and ought still strive. But the proof of that view would,

Human Progress

I confess, have to be very strong in order to overcome a repugnance I feel towards it. I wonder how many people there are whose enthusiasm for a good cause would be in no degree dashed by the discovery that all effort and all self-sacrifice on its behalf would never achieve more than an evanescent result in the world about them.

It may be well, perhaps, not to make our enthusiasm too dependent upon the realization of our visions. There is something heroic, no doubt, in Tyrrell's ideal of the worker, who has no hope of success, and yet works on with indomitable resolution, because he sees that that is good. The hope of realizing a splendid vision may prompt fine action, but there is more promise in the temper which lays less stress upon the hope, and more upon the determination to labour, whether the end be achieved or not. Yet it is impossible not to be interested in the question whether there is any likelihood of such labour being effectual in the present sphere. Personally, I do not think we need be shut up to the pessimism of Marcus Aurelius, of the material scientists, and of George Tyrrell. One cannot, it is true, argue from one's certainty of a Divine Purpose an equal certainty that human progress on this planet will go on. But if we believe in a Divine Purpose, then we must hold that the progress of humanity hitherto, from the brute to primitive man, from primitive man to civilized man, has been part of God's design. And if God's design has up till now meant a gradual ascent of man on this planet, that is surely, so far as it goes, a reason for anticipating that God's design will involve an analogous ascent from stage to stage in the future. This globe may be only the platform which mankind crosses, and the true history of mankind may

Hellenism and Christianity

follow the line of his passage into the Unseen, not the succession of generations upon the earth. Granted, and yet the earth too, as the sacred vehicle of man's spirit in this phase of its being, may have a history of its own, guided to a worthy end.

One must face the assertion that life will become impossible upon the planet after a limited term of years. If the scientific view is right, which foresees an extinction of life under the stress of cold or heat or drought, this means not only that the history of the race cannot go on beyond that point, but that the final extinction of the last man will be preceded by ages of decline, ages during which man will wage an ever losing battle with Nature. My own feeling with regard to a pessimism based on such an anticipation is that all forecasts our science can at present make with regard to such a remote future must be extremely doubtful. How, for instance, could any calculation based upon the natural forces in play upon the globe, before the appearance of life, have ever forecast the marvel of life and its developments in beast and man ? And how do we know what may not be produced by new spiritual forces, entering into the present world, as organic life entered the world of mechanical nature ? There has been, at any rate, a movement of thought in our time towards emphasizing the elasticity of life, the scope of initiative, the freshness of things really new, the incalculable possibilities of the future.

XI

THE PROBLEM OF ESCHATOLOGY

A GREAT deal of controversy has gone on during recent years as to the place occupied by eschatology in the teaching of our Lord—how far His whole teaching was dependent upon a particular view of the end of the world, especially a belief in its immediacy and suddenness, how far the eschatological elements were something subordinate and detachable, leaving the main body of His teaching very much as it would be without them. On this controversy I do not now propose to enter. Whether eschatological views occupied a principal, or a subordinate, place in our Lord's teaching, it is admitted on both sides that they are there. And we may extend the phrase " our Lord's teaching " to cover the belief of the primitive Church. For it is also a debatable question how far in the gospels, as they lie before us, we have the words of Christ as He spoke them with His lips, and how far they have been supplemented from the belief and practice of the primitive community. I do not propose to examine this question either, and it is the less necessary for my purpose to try to draw any hard and fast line between the actual teaching of Christ and the belief and practice of the community, as we hold that the activity of Christ

Hellenism and Christianity

in the Church did not cease with His bodily removal, but that much in subsequent belief and practice has been indeed the inspiration of His ever-present Spirit in the community animated by His risen life.

We start then simply with the fact that the teaching of Christ and the faith of the primitive Church included a body of conceptions as to the end of the world-process —an end which is described as the Return, the Advent, of Christ Himself. This body of conceptions has continued to form part of the Christian tradition up to the present day, part of the tradition which we took up as our heritage in childhood. It is perfectly true that the expectation of Christ's return became less absorbing and intense as the first generations of Christians passed away with the hope unfulfilled, that it began to be relegated into a more distant future, and sink into the background of thought. It is also true that the details of the future drama have been differently conceived and arranged at various times and by various interpreters of the Bible. But in all ages, pronounced or faint, the expectation has been there, and through all varieties certain features had been constant, up to our own time. There had been a general agreement of Christendom from the first to the nineteenth centuries, that the world-process would be consummated in a cosmic event or a cosmic drama, whereby every individual who had died upon the planet would pass from the state of a disembodied spirit to that of a spirit indued with bodily organs—the Resurrection of the Body, *Resurrectio Carnis*—and would be confronted with Jesus Christ as Judge.

Such had been the uniform belief of the Church up to the last few generations. It is admitted that during

The Problem of Eschatology

the last hundred years the current view of the world-process has been profoundly changed. Looking backward the modern man no longer believes that the history of man began from a single pair in 4004 B.C., or that the old story of the Garden and the Snake is literal historical fact. Instead of abrupt beginnings, he sees everywhere processes of gradual development, going back in the case of the human race to an antiquity so remote as to make everything since the Pyramids recent. Modern theology has accommodated itself to the change, and we no longer find a difficulty in recognizing a Divine Purpose in development, just as our fathers saw it in abrupt creations. A literature of Christian thought upon modern lines has grown up and become popular, so that younger Christians of to-day no longer, in looking backward, are perplexed, as their fathers were, with the problem of reconciling " Moses and Geology." Those old difficulties seem to lie far behind us now. But the change of general view bears not only upon the past, but upon the future, and while with regard to the past modern Christianity has achieved a generally accepted re-construction, much less thought seems to me to have been given to the problem, what re-construction of the traditional view as to the future does the modern world-view entail ?

We still keep the traditional imagery in our liturgies and hymns—the vast and vivid drama to which the expectation of the Church turned age after age—the still night shattered by a trumpet, the shout of the archangel, the Divine Figure seated upon clouds, the gravestones thrust upwards, the sea giving up the dead which is in it, a Throne and unnumbered multitudes gathered before it, a new heaven and new earth. We probably were

singing last Advent some of the familiar hymns, a version
of the medieval Latin :—

> Hora novissima, tempora pessima sunt ; vigilemus.
> ecce minaciter imminet arbiter ille supremus ;
> imminet, imminet, ut mala terminet, aequa coronet,
> recta remuneret, anxia liberet, aethera donet—

Or,

> Great God, what do I see and hear ?
> The end of things created !
> The Judge of Mankind doth appear
> On clouds of glory seated—

Or,

> Lo, He comes with clouds descending,
> Once for favoured sinners slain,
> Thousand thousand saints attending
> Swell the triumph of His train.

Now I want to ask what does all that really mean to
us to-day ? It seems to me important to ask, because
nothing tends more to make religion unreal than to maintain forms which have lost their meaning for us. What do
we mean when we sing those hymns ?

That we do not understand it all literally is, of course,
immediately obvious. Even our fathers did not take
every detail literally. At any rate, I suppose few educated
Christians since the Middle Ages have supposed that the
last trump was a metal instrument measuring so many
inches, or that our Lord would appear at a point of the
cloudy atmosphere so definitely fixed in space as to be
invisible to persons upon the other hemisphere. Every
one would admit that the reality was clothed to some
extent in images which had a symbolical, and not
a literal, value. The question is, How far does the
symbolism go ?

The Problem of Eschatology

It may perhaps be said : " We cannot tell. This is the traditional imagery. It covers some great indescribable reality. The symbolism takes us as close to it as our faculties can come. We know it is not literal fact, but we cannot get beyond it." Can we consider this answer satisfactory ? In the first place, it does not seem to me that the symbolism would have any value for us, unless we had some sort of notion, it may be an indistinct and groping one, of what it stood for. There are symbols which stand for something else by an arbitrary convention —a visible mark, for instance, for a vocal sound, such as the letters of an alphabet, or a palm branch signifying victory. There is no resemblance between the symbol and the thing symbolized. There are other symbols whose value is based upon a resemblance. It is not an absolute resemblance. There are features in which the symbol is unlike the thing symbolized, as well as features in which they are alike. Let us take an example—a lion as the symbol of a brave man. Now in this case, knowing both the symbol and the thing symbolized, we are able to compare them and see both the points of resemblance and the points of difference. Thenceforth, in taking the lion as the symbol of the brave man we are able to attend to the points of resemblance, certain mental aptitudes in the lion, and disregard the other qualities of the lion, its bodily shape, colour, and so on. The case is different where something is proffered us as the symbol of a reality *which we do not know*. Obviously, if it were a symbol of the first kind, one standing for the reality by an arbitrary convention and bearing no resemblance to it, it would be absolutely valueless to us. But neither has it any value for us, if it resembles the reality,

Hellenism and Christianity

unless we have some sort of notion in which of its features the resemblance lies and which are accidental. Suppose a brave man were an unknown something : you set the lion as a symbol before me, and say : " Look at this, the brave man is something like this." Well, I gain little unless I know that it is those particular mental qualities in the lion which I have to take as my guide ; otherwise I might equally well form my idea of the brave man from the lion's mane and claws.

In the second place, we could not affirm with such confidence that the images presented to us were symbolical, or partially symbolical, unless we had some notion of what the reality must be. We are sure, for instance, that the reality is of a nature to exclude a literal trumpet of metal. But that is already to know something about it. In other words, we could not detect the merely symbolical character of any representation, unless our thought could in some way reach beyond the symbol and contrast it with the reality. This knowledge of the reality may be of a very inarticulate and formless kind. It is possible to have a knowledge of something which we cannot bring into clear consciousness and which yet directs us. A familiar case is where we know a name, but cannot, as we say, call it to mind for the moment. Let somebody suggest any other name, and we unhesitatingly repel it ; we know it is not that : the blank in our mind, as I think James puts it somewhere, is a very *active blank* ; it refuses energetically. Perhaps in the same way in the case of a symbol representing to us some transcendent Reality, we may have no clear image of what the Reality is, though we feel sure that this feature in the symbol does not belong to it, whilst in that feature we touch something essential.

The Problem of Eschatology

We may turn, then—nay, we are bound to turn—to this traditional body of images covered by the terms Second Advent, Resurrection of the Body, Last Judgement, End of the World, and try to distinguish the accidents of the symbol from the Reality which it adumbrates. But first it would be well for us to consider what has become, so far as one can judge by sermons and current religious phraseology, the ordinary modification which the Christian hope has undergone in the minds of educated Christians to-day. The great characteristic, as we saw, of the nineteenth century thought was that it replaced the idea of abrupt transitions by the idea of continuous progressive development. The traditional Christian eschatology represented the coming of Christ in judgement, the coming of the kingdom in power, as something abrupt and catastrophic, a Divine intervention suddenly breaking in upon a world which, so far from evolving towards the goal, had sunk into ever deeper darkness with time. " *Hora novissima, tempora pessima sunt, vigilemus.*"

From such a conception modern thought has swerved away. For the final coming of Christ in judgement we are given a progressive coming of Christ in history, a series of Divine acts of judgement, in the fall of Jerusalem, the fall of the Roman Empire, the French Revolution, and so on. The kingdom of God is now a spiritual and moral condition of mankind to be gradually brought about by human effort. It is common to hear missions spoken of as " spreading God's Kingdom," or the establishment of the Kingdom upon earth spoken of as the consummation to which the work of the Church, social and religious, is destined to lead. What the conditions of life upon the planet will be, when the Kingdom is established, and how long such a state of things can go on—for presumably life upon the planet must end some day—upon these points one gets no light from current phraseology. Earnest curates perpetually quote that verse of Blake's in support of the visions of Christian Socialism !

> I will not cease from mental strife,
>   Nor shall my sword sleep in my hand,
> Till I have built Jerusalem
>   In England's green and pleasant land.

In the primitive Christian conception, Jerusalem was not built by any man upon the earth. It descended, adorned already as a bride, out of heaven.

The modern Christian therefore retains from the primitive eschatology the assurance that the history of mankind upon this planet is destined to end in a state of bliss, although he has altered his imaginative conception of the way in which that state of bliss is to be brought about. Any primitive Christian who looked for a sudden and miraculous establishment of God's Kingdom, a convulsion of nature, was, according to this view, right in hoping for a future " divine event," but wrong in his picture of its circumstances. But upon what did the primitive Christian base his hope ? Upon what he took to be a prophetic revelation, a prediction delivered upon God's authority. This surely makes a difficulty for the modern view.

For the one thing which it may appear illogical to do with a Divine oracle is to emend it by human ingenuity, and continue to put it forth as based upon Divine authority. You may question its authenticity, its authority as a whole, but you can, it may be said, hardly alter it in parts and leave the rest authoritative.

The Problem of Eschatology

The fact is, I believe, that the modern man would feel reluctant to base even that part of the primitive hope which he retains upon the bare declaration of a prophet. It may well be that the dogmatic assurance with which the old " naturalist " anti-Christian denied that " miracles " could occur, in the sense—so far as you *can* make sense out of confused thinking—that we could take pretty complete stock of the laws of Nature and know that certain things were impossible under all circumstances —it may well be that this assurance is not quite so robust or so widely diffused to-day even in circles outside Christianity. But it seems that even if we are more ready to admit on principle something for which the popular term " miracle " may be used, the tendency of the modern man is to reduce the miraculous to as narrow limits as possible. A sudden coming of Christ, which involved an absolute breach in the physical world, would be miracle on a gigantic scale, and we prefer the idea of a gradual and orderly development. But prediction itself—in so far as it entails supernatural intuition of the future not logically inferred from existing data—prediction itself belongs to the sphere popularly considered miraculous. And I doubt whether " Modern Churchmen " would give, as the reason of their hope for the race, a recorded prediction. If we had asked the early Christian why he believed that Christ would come upon the clouds, he would have been ready at once to answer, " Because God has said so." If our neighbour asked us why we looked forward to a blissful future for the earth, should we be content with an answer so simple ?

Perhaps we should not feel quite clear as to how far all the predictions contained in the New Testament are to be regarded as statements made by God Himself, infallible through and through. One thing surely is plain. We cannot consider the predictions of the New Testament apart from the older prophetical literature of Israel. They are the same in kind with it, and we must interpret them by laws which appertain to the *genus* as a whole. This the traditional view did, and just because it did so, the great change of view which has come about with regard to the prophets of old Israel must affect the traditional view of New Testament prophecy.

To the early Christian, perhaps we might say to Christians generally up to the nineteenth century, the predictive element was the important thing in Old Testament prophecy. They saw details, which could have been known beforehand by nothing but miraculous revelation, stated with unquestionable distinctness. Now beside the general tendency of the modern world to be shy of prediction as something miraculous, the result of the actual critical study of the Old Testament has been to reduce the predictive element in a signal way. To our fathers Cyrus had been prophesied of by name some one hundred and fifty years before his birth ; it is now generally admitted that the chapters of Isaiah which refer to Cyrus were composed in the time of the conqueror. To our fathers Daniel, living under Nebuchadnezzar and Cyrus, had given a detailed sketch of the wars and alliances of Greek kings many centuries later ; it is now generally admitted that the book of Daniel was composed in the reign of Antiochus Epiphanes. And so on in many other instances. It is only natural, then, when modern theology asks us to

The Problem of Eschatology

look upon the Hebrew prophets, not so much as predictors, but as preachers of righteousness. Their real office, it is said, was not to foretell the future, but to declare, in the modern phrase, moral and spiritual *values*. The advantage of this view to the modern man is that the gift of spiritual insight given to the prophets now becomes, not something miraculous, a faculty of immediate *clairvoyance*, but a gift of insight into spiritual values the same in kind as that possessed by every good man, only raised to an exceptional intensity. There seems no inherent nexus between spiritual goodness and miraculous prevision; we do not see that a man in proportion to his goodness possesses the faculty of foreseeing the future; but we do see that a man in proportion to his goodness has a sensitiveness to spiritual values, and there is therefore no difficulty in the idea of spiritual geniuses, of persons who read the moral and spiritual qualities in the life of their times with exceptional vividness and truth.

Personally, I must confess that I do not find the view which entirely dismisses the predictive element in the Hebrew prophets, which treats them simply as preachers of righteousness, a satisfactory one. We must certainly allow that modern research has reduced the predictive element to very much narrower proportions than our fathers imagined. We must probably allow that some of the concrete predictions in the Old Testament were proved mistaken by the event. But to suppress the predictive element in prophecy altogether—do we realize what that means?

Let us here call to mind the distinction now commonly drawn between what are called " existential judgements " and judgements of value. An existential judgement simply asserts the existence of some fact—its existence past, present, or future ; a judgement of value asserts that something is good or beautiful, that it *ought* to be or *ought not* to be. Now the point which it is needful to grasp first is that neither from premises which are all existential judgements can we infer logically, infer without a leap over a logical chasm, a judgement of value, nor from premises which are all value-judgements can we infer, without a similar leap, a judgement of existence. It will be plain what this means if one takes an instance of the former sort of attempt. Our moral judgements, our assertions that this or that is right or wrong, are value-judgements, and it has been thought in some quarters that our moral judgements, the deliverances of our conscience as it is to-day, could be proved true or false by a scientific research into the history of their development. It has been thought that you could have a moral law based upon natural science. But scientific research taken by itself could issue only in a series of existential judgements, a series of statements that this or that was, or had been, a matter of fact ; no possible piling up, no complication, of such statements, could yield any conclusion as to what *ought to be* or *have been*. To get such a conclusion you have to interpolate somewhere among the premises a judgement of value—such a judgement, for example, as that pleasure or the survival of the race is the end which *ought* to be pursued—and the moment you interpolate such a premise you are making a leap.

But it is equally true that from no series of value-judgements can you infer that anything has, is, or will be the case as a matter of fact. Our value-judgements express what we believe ought to be the case, the demands of our moral or our æsthetic sense. But from these, taken by themselves, we cannot infer anything as to what existed or exists and is going to exist in the objective world as a matter of fact. To do that we have to interpolate among our value-judgements an existential judgement that Reality is actually of a kind to satisfy the demands of our hearts. This again is to make a leap. But to make this leap seems to be just what all religion does; it seems the essence of religious faith. Of course the question may be asked whether we are justified in making it; whether it would not be wiser to stick to what is logically demonstrable; and to answer that question is to embark on the whole theory of religion. For the moment it may be held allowable to take it for granted that we *are* justified in making the leap of religious faith, only saying that if one had to set forth the justification, presumably one would urge that even all demonstration was ultimately based on faith—the faith that the universe so far met the demands of our own natures as to be rational; and secondly, that we were, as it seems, compelled by the necessity of acting to make some sort of leap; whether we wanted to do so or no, we were pushed by the advance of time, moment by moment, to will something, and we could not will without some working hypothesis as to the world in which our action was to take effect.

We cannot reduce religion to a mass of value-judgements and nothing more; it involves the great existential judgement: The Reality, which my heart tells me ought to be, *is*. God is. But obviously the Reality, which my heart tells me ought to be, is not, if my vision of the world is limited to what I see now. Faith therefore asserts that if I could see the whole of Reality, the whole time-process, whose still future tracts will determine what the value of this Past and Present is (just as the still future bars of music may make a discord good), if I could see the whole time-process, I should see what ought to be, existing. That is why religion involves essentially the element of prediction. It never can stop at declaring a value, it must go on to declare that the time-process in its future tracts will satisfy the demand which I am led by my perception of value to make. However much you may strive to reduce Religion to its barest skeleton, you cannot get rid of the predictive element. Take the religious philosophy enunciated by Höffding. He wants to throw off everything which looks like an ecclesiastical dogma. He discharges the specific elements of Christianity. But that is not enough. Belief in a *personal* God must go. Even the language which Sabatier uses of God, speaking of Him *as* personal, seems superstitious to Höffding. And so we get, as the real essence of religion, a belief in the " conservation of values." You could hardly reduce religion to a thinner abstraction than that. But note that the predictive element is still there. Faith in the conservation of values is faith that the future part of the time-process will actually be of such a character that the values I perceive will be conserved.

When to a mass of value-judgements, judgements which are based upon spiritual perception, you add the existential judgement which is the postulate of faith, immediately those value-judgements have a bearing upon the future course of the world. The Hebrew prophets did

The Problem of Eschatology

not only declare " This is righteous," " That is evil," but they asserted strongly that the Power working in history would shape future events in reference to the distinction between righteousness and evil-doing.   History had a spiritual purpose.   Of course, it is possible to regard them as right in this conviction, without holding them to have been right as to the exact way in which they painted imaginatively the course of future events.

We are familiar with the two motives which constitute the predictive part of the Old Testament prophets.   One might say, indeed, that their predictions are little more than variations, according to the circumstances of the time and the dramatic imagery suggested to the prophet, upon those two themes.   There is the declaration of impending judgement, the declaration that upon the evil-doers whom the prophet denounces will fall a judgement of Jehovah, an annihilating destruction, and there is, secondly, the declaration that the people of Israel will after that time of tribulation be restored in a state of bliss and righteousness.   Both these themes are filled out with different imaginative colouring—the destruction is connected with a particular foreign Power, the Assyrian or the Babylonian ; sometimes the invasion is described in literal terms, sometimes in metaphoric language, as a flood, fire, or devastating wind.   The future state of bliss, again, is presented in a variety of sensible images —the peace between the lion and the ox, the glorified city of Jerusalem, the reigning house of David represented by wise and righteous kings.   Even, therefore, if we adopt the view which rules out from prophetic inspiration anything like miraculous *clairvoyance*, we must admit a large predictive element.   Only on that view the prediction would not be an immediate intuition of the future, but a deduction instinctively made from the combination of a mass of value-judgements, of perceptions, with the judgement, no longer a matter of perception, but of faith, that the course of the world would actually be guided in accordance with those values. The prophet *saw* unrighteousness, and feeling that the only way in which the course of events could adjust the moral anomaly was for the unrighteous people to be abolished out of the land, he asserted confidently that this would happen. The prophet *saw* in the religious tradition of his people something of unique value, and he felt that the only way the course of the world could correspond with what ought to be, was for the treasure possessed by Israel to be saved and exalted in power, and so he predicted confidently that the nation could not perish altogether in the judgement, that it was reserved for a glorious future.

The inspiration of the prophets, on this view, was limited to quickening, first, their *perceptions* of spiritual qualities, of what was good and bad in the life of their times, and secondly, making strong and bold their *faith* that the course of the world was guided by Some One who cared for righteousness. But can we really be sure that it was nothing more than this? May it not be that those are too hasty who would rule out every kind of miraculous prevision? If we compare the predictions of Isaiah, Jeremiah, Ezekiel, with the event we get, it seems to me, a measure of correspondence which it is hard to account for, if the prophets were going simply upon a faith that the course of the world would somehow justify their moral judgements. Isaiah and Jeremiah both

The Problem of Eschatology

declared that the true Israel would survive the judgement, and this alone might be taken as a deduction from the premise of faith, of which we have been speaking. But they did more than this; Isaiah declared that the Assyrian king would not take Jerusalem, and Sennacherib failed to do so; Jeremiah declared that the Babylonian *would* destroy Jerusalem, and Nebuchadnezzar did so. Perhaps the picture of the suffering Servant in the 53rd chapter of Isaiah remains the strongest instance of all. You may say that the writer knew by spiritual experience and insight the redemptive value of suffering, and therefore threw upon the mists of the future his ideal figure of One suffering for the sins of the people. Personally, I find it difficult to read that passage and think that such an explanation gives the whole of the matter. I find it difficult to believe that some immediate intuition of the future Reality did not here guide the mind of the writer, that it was only a case of his making a forward conjectural leap into the future from the basis of his own experience, and not rather a case of that which was still part of the unfulfilled purpose of God shining directly upon him. At the same time the correspondence of events with predictions does not seem to have been exact in all particulars; the Assyrian invasion, for instance, did not apparently follow the line of march described by Isaiah in anticipation: while Ezekiel was right in predicting that Nebuchadnezzar would take Jerusalem, his prediction that the same king would take Tyre was, as he admits himself in chapter xxix, verse 18, not fulfilled. To me personally, what these facts suggest is that the inspiration of the prophets did include some sort of immediate intuition or adumbration of the future, something

Hellenism and Christianity

"supernatural," but an intuition which became to some extent contaminated in the human medium with accidental conjectures and images.

The great Hebrew prophets, however, were not the immediate predecessors of the New Testament writers. Between them lay that extensive literature called Apocalyptic, which was a characteristic product of the later centuries of Judaism. In the Old Testament Canon it is represented for us by the book of Daniel, and possibly by fragments interpolated in the older prophetic books; outside the Canon it is represented more voluminously by Enoch and other books. In form, the difference between the apocalyptic writings and the older prophets is striking; prose has largely taken the place of poetry; the vague metaphors and similes have been given hard and fast outlines, the events of the future drama are arranged and articulated, the actors have become concrete angelic or demonic personalities, with individual names, Michael, Raphael, Azazel. Under the difference of form, there is, however, more similarity of principle than might appear at first. Here, too, the writer is moved by a perception of spiritual values. The ungodly man of the apocalyptic writers is not indeed quite the same sort of person as the unrighteous man of Isaiah or Jeremiah, but he has a great deal in common with him, and there is in both cases on the part of the writer an ardent antagonism to what he sees as sin. The prediction of the apocalyptic writer may also be regarded as an imaginative expression of the faith that present moral anomalies will be adjusted by the future course of the world, and adjusted by a judgement which will discern between the righteous and the wicked. So far the apocalyptic writers render the theme of the prophets in another form. But there *are* differences beside the difference of form.

I suppose one would say the great difference is that the vision of the apocalyptic writers extends, not only outside the land of Israel, but outside the sphere of this world altogether. The Judgement is to be a cosmic event reaching to all mankind, even the dead generations ; the final state of the righteous and wicked is not to be found in a purified Davidic kingdom in Palestine, but in a non-terrestrial heaven and hell. Hence, the individual character of the judgement is emphasized. Every human soul is to appear at the Divine judgement-seat and be judged according to his or her works. This new transcendental outlook is combined in various ways in different writings with the old earthly outlook of the great prophets of the past. A restored Israelite kingdom in the actual Palestine is still normally expected, but now as something transient and provisional, preceding the final state of bliss or misery in another world. The agent again through whom the Lord will act in the future judgement and deliverance, the Messiah, is prominent in a new way. To the old prophets, Jehovah was thought of as acting Himself in the character of Judge and Saviour, no human or human-divine intermediary coming into view ; in most of the apocalyptic writers the Lord acts through the Messiah. The writing which gives the highest place to the Messiah is that forming part of the Book of Enoch—chapters xxxvii to lxx.

The Messiah is here a Heavenly Being, described as the Elect One or the Son of Man, present with the Father from the beginning of human history, but known only to those among men to whom He had been mystically

Hellenism and Christianity

revealed. It is He, this Son of Man, who according to the writing in question is to be the future Judge, not only of all mankind, but of the angels, and who is to be manifest upon earth among its redeemed and glorified inhabitants, when the wicked have been purged out of it. According to Dr. Charles the date of this writing is some two or three generations before the birth of Jesus.

All this apocalyptic material was current when our Lord was on the earth and when the primitive Church formulated its hopes. We cannot understand the apocalyptic element in the Gospels, in the Epistles, and in the Book of Revelation, except in relation to it. As a matter of fact, with the exception of one modification, one vastly important modification, I do not know whether there is anything either in the discourses of Christ or in Saint Paul or in the Revelation which does not belong to the current apocalyptic tradition. With the exception of one modification, Christianity took over a mass of that tradition unchanged. But the one modification gave it all a different note. For the Person who was to be God's agent in the future Judgement and Redemption was identified with Jesus Himself. It was no longer an ideal figure, cloudy and abstract, for whom the Christian looked up at the night sky, but Some One whom he knew, Some One with all the inexpressible richness, the penetrant appeal of a Living Person. It was not only some deliverer he longed for, to adjust the wrongs of the world, but the Friend whose touch he had felt, for whom his orphaned heart cried out, without whom, having once known Him, he could never be happy again. It was with a very different inner meaning that the Spirit and the Bride said " Come "—" Lord Jesus, come quickly."

The Problem of Eschatology

To the writer of those chapters of Enoch the idea of standing before the Judgement-Seat of the Son of Man cannot have conveyed all that it meant to the early disciple to stand before the Judgement-Seat of Christ.

When we now come back to our original question—What the Advent imagery means for us—how far our anticipations of the future are to be determined by it, I feel that the answer must be according to the view we take of all this later Jewish and early Christian apocalyptic literature. If we take the view that it was inspired simply by a perception of spiritual values and a faith-judgement that the course of the world would be regulated in reference to them, then we accept what we accept, not on an authority exterior to ourselves, but so far as our own perceptions of spiritual value confirm its teaching, and we are prepared ourselves to adopt the hypothesis of faith. If, however, we believe that there is in it any measure of miraculous prevision, then just in that measure we must accept it on authority, since obviously a prediction based upon a faculty which we do not possess ourselves is one which we cannot directly check. It is then only a question of the grounds on which we attribute this supernatural faculty to the apocalyptic writers, just as in the case of any one now claiming to possess a power of *clairvoyance*, we should believe on his authority any prediction which we could not check, according as in other cases he had proved veridical.

It is at this point I am obliged to launch out into tentative suggestions in a field to which little systematic thought has so far been given and where one's individual scheme must have a query attached to it. I can only speak for myself.

I feel then that even without the supposition of any

Hellenism and Christianity

miraculous prevision what is essential for the Christian faith can be drawn from the values concerned—combined, of course, with the general premise of faith that the conservation of spiritual values will be secured. The elements making up our hope on this basis would, I think, be the following :—

1. The unique value of each human individual may, I suppose, be held to have been the determining considera-tion, consciously or unconsciously, in the belief that every individual would sooner or later be brought before the Divine judgement-seat. And this belief is surely con-firmed by our own perceptions. Do we not feel that if the world is really organized on moral principles, the soul which has chosen unrighteousness rather than God must sooner or later come to a consciousness of its condition in the light of God's character, with the attendant pain ? And this seems to give one what is essential in the doctrine of the Last Judgement on its sterner side.

2. There is the conviction on the other side that the values included in the spiritual life point forward to vast possibilities which remain unrealized in this life. They are apprehensions inchoate and fragmentary, and the world is not really a moral world, if they have no future expansion beyond death. This seems to me the essential element in the doctrine of the reward of the righteous.

3. But there are two things which any idea of future bliss implies, if it is true to the values inherent in the spiritual life. First, it must imply no impoverishment of individual personality, but an enlargement and an increased power of self-expression. Our bodies here are the organs of our self-expression and inter-communica-tion, imperfect organs enough. The belief that they will

The Problem of Eschatology

be superseded by far more perfect modes of expression seems to me what is essential in the doctrine of the Resurrection of the Body.

Secondly, any future bliss must be social. This is implied in the innermost character of the spiritual life. Love itself, the highest of values, implies a society. Perhaps in no way do we feel the unsatisfactoriness of our present state more than in the narrow limits to intercourse, the impossibility of knowing, and therefore of loving, except within a very small range, the broken, distorted nature of our best knowledge of each other. The idea of a society in which the possibilities of knowing and loving are extended beyond anything we can conceive in our present conditions—that seems to me the essential thing in the doctrine of the Church Triumphant, of Heaven.

4. Lastly, there is the specific hope of the Christian, the hope of " being with Christ," of " seeing Him as He is." Here again we know the value of Christ by experience, and to us any Heaven without Him would not be Heaven. It is possible that to minds of a strongly mystical cast the present communion with Christ is so intense that there seems no possibility left unrealized. But for the ordinary struggling disciple the negative side of experience here is only too constantly present, " Whom *not* having seen," " through a glass, darkly," " present in the body, and absent from the Lord."

It seems to me that even without supposing any miraculous prevision of the conditions of the future life in the apocalyptic writers, the Christian hope, so far as concerns the elements just described, is dictated by what we actually perceive of the values constituting the spiritual

Hellenism and Christianity

life coupled with the postulate of faith. But one need not therefore rule out a measure of direct prevision as a possibility. It is all a question whether the apocalyptic writers, where we can check them in the past, show a measure of prescience greater than can be probably accounted for by a perception of spiritual values alone. And if we hold the Christian estimate of Christ, we may perhaps see such a measure of prescience in the chapters of Enoch dealing with the Son of Man, just as we may surely see it in the Suffering Servant of Isaiah liii. If this is so, we may draw a hope for the future of the race upon this planet from the apocalyptic anticipation of a Millennium. We need not regard a belief in the future progress or happiness of mankind on this earth as an essential part of Christian belief ; in those elements of the Christian hope which were put forward as being inferences from our present perception of values, a hope for the race upon earth was not included. But one may still cherish a hope for this earth, and such hope is confirmed by the possibility that in their anticipation of a Millennium the apocalyptic writers had a ray of *clairvoyance.* After all, the history of Man on this planet has got to end somehow, and it seems to me " worthy of God," if I may use the phrase, that even in this sphere good should triumph. The early Christians believed in a future reign of Christ upon this earth, which was not to be eternal (as indeed the earth is not eternal), but was to precede the eternal state. This belief, called Chiliasm, it is the fashion among modern theologians to speak of slightingly as unspiritual. I cannot conceive why, unless you are a Docetist and believe the Incarnation to be unspiritual. If the literal presence of Christ upon the earth 1900

The Problem of Eschatology

years ago is a fact of great spiritual importance, I cannot see why the belief in His presence upon earth at some future age should be unspiritual. But how can we conceive such a presence? We are in the region of imaginative conjecture, and a fancy of mine may go for what it is worth. We have two records in the New Testament of people seeing the heavenly Christ, the case of Stephen and the case of Paul. There have been, since then, alleged appearances of Christ throughout the ages of Christianity. Especially, the number of people who have declared that they saw Christ just before death has been remarkable. Now supposing these appearances were, all or some of them, the real perception of the living Christ, and supposing in some future state of mankind, its spiritual education having gone much further than it has gone to-day, such a sensible presence of Christ to men were not something occasional and rare, but something normal and common in the lives of all, would not that be indeed the Return of the Lord?

XII

REASON AND DOGMA

THERE is, I suppose, no statement which has been commoner in theology than that the truths of religion are not amenable to human " reason." " The thing is certain just because it is impossible "—the defiant outburst of Tertullian 1,700 years ago. " A fool is he who hopes that our reason can run along the infinite road pursued by One Substance in Three Persons "—words which Dante puts into the mouth of his Virgil. And it is not only within the Christian Church that such things have been said. Tertullian after all was only echoing the arguments of the pre-Christian pagan scepticism which had defended the practice of the old religion, with all its apparent absurdities, by throwing doubt on the validity of reason. And in our own day we know of anti-intellectualist forms of philosophy which discredit reason as against feeling and instinct, and so offer a tempting alliance to the Christian apologist—an alliance of which some Christians have not been slow to avail themselves—whether wisely or not, is the question. I have heard of modern Indians defending their traditional religious practices and beliefs against Christian criticism on similar lines.

Reason and Dogma

It appears to me that both those who attack religious doctrines in the name of " reason," and those who defend them by discrediting " reason," habitually use this term without any clear conception of what they mean by it. " Reason," they say, " teaches one thing ; dogma affirms the contrary." Reason, I submit, on the other hand, teaches us nothing at all—or rather it teaches us only one thing which cannot by itself conflict with any religious or anti-religious dogma, unless such dogma can be shown to involve a logical self-contradiction.

Perhaps we ought first to notice that the alleged conflict between reason and religious dogmas is of two kinds. There are first the cases in which the propositions maintained by the Church are said to involve in themselves or between each other a logical absurdity or self-contradiction. The doctrine of the Trinity, as stated in the Athanasian Creed, is the typical example. There are, secondly, cases in which the religious dogma affirms that a particular event took place, whereas reason, it is said, teaches that such an event did not take place. These cases are comprised under the term " miracles." They must be carefully distinguished from cases of the first kind. The proposition here does not involve any conception which is in itself unintelligible or self-contradictory. There is no *logical* absurdity in the proposition, A Virgin bore a son, or A Man walked on the water. These propositions have a perfectly clear meaning and present to our apprehension a consistent picture. Only, as a matter of fact, reason teaches—so we are told—that these events did not take place.

What is " reason " ? If we use the term in the proper sense, it is the consistency between the different factors of experience or the mental activity by which we apprehend that consistency. The one and only thing that reason teaches is: "There is a consistency between the factors of experience, whatever they may be." But it says nothing at all as to what the factors of experience, as a matter of fact, are. Because we are reasonable beings, we are sure, to start with, that there is a consistency between all the factors of our experience, if only we can find it. And so, since our experience, as it comes to us, often seems chaotic, our reason never rests till we have discovered the scheme which makes our experience a consistent whole. The problem is always being renewed, because new bits of experience are always coming to us, and very often the new bit won't at all fit into the scheme we have ready. Then the scheme has to be modified and remade to take in the new datum. Our convictions about the universe at any moment are the result of our piecemeal experience as worked up and co-ordinated by our reason. We express these convictions in definite statements. Of course in one way the convictions and the statements expressing them go beyond our experience. They give, not only experience we have actually had, but the logical scheme we have devised to hold together the different bits of our experience. That scheme is a framework, part of which is filled with actual experience, part of which is hypothetical construction, bridging over the gaps, an empty framework, into which we believe that experience would have fitted, if we had had an opportunity of putting things to proof by direct perception at that point, or that fresh experience will fit when it comes. Sometimes, when it comes, it does fit straight away into the framework. Then our rational scheme is, so far verified. Sometimes it refuses to fit. Then it shows that our scheme has been in part constructed of false hypothesis.

It is no doubt in this sense that some people describe a particular religious doctrine as contrary to " reason." They imply that they know well enough all the data of experience out of which the belief was made, and hence are able to affirm confidently that the belief was wrongly made, not according to the laws of sound logic. But what if the difference of the belief in question from their own belief is not due to the logical machine having worked differently upon the same data, but to its having worked upon different data, upon another mass of experience ? If there is any possibility of this, of data having come in which lie outside the range of their experience, or of data which, though they are within their experience, they have failed to attend to or appreciate, then we might expect them to show some diffidence in affirming that the belief is unreasonable. And when we are dealing with religious belief, with belief as to the inner reality of the universe, it seems somewhat bold to assume that there can be no data before any one else except those included in the range of one's own individual experience.

All around the little experience of each one of us, the little number of things we remember having seen and heard and felt, is a vast world of things existing and happening. We are immensely concerned to know something of this environment, because it is obvious that the significance of our own small lives and the right conduct of our own lives depend upon the context of our lives in the world as a whole. If we could never have any knowledge of anything except what we individually have experienced, we should be like people in a closed motor-car at night, lit up inside but rushing on without any light to pierce the surrounding darkness; a wreck would come very soon. As a matter of fact, the greatest number of things which fill our consciousness, which make up our world, are things we have never directly experienced; we are conscious, for instance, of London with its millions of lives all round us, and England round London, and the world with its problems, impoverished Europe, Bolshevist Russia, India, China, outside England. It is important to us to know thousands of things we can never directly experience. How do we get from the limited data of our experience to a knowledge of what lies outside of it? It is here reason comes in. Although reason by itself tells us nothing, if you give reason the data of our experience to operate with, it takes us beyond them by applying to them its one doctrine: " The universe, or experience as a whole, is consistent." Our experience is part of a world-wide pattern, and we can therefore infer from the part we have seen what the rest is which we have not seen.

Wherever there is uniform recurrence, as in a row of columns, there is a pattern. In our own personal experience we discover from babyhood onwards numberless uniformities—the effect of burning when we put anything into the fire, the sinking of the stone and the floating of the stick in water. Whenever we have registered a uniformity we take this to be one of the characteristics of the world-pattern and assume that it holds good all over the rest of the world which we have not seen.

And now note that we are continually from babyhood correcting our theory of the pattern according to fresh experience. We find it to be a much less simple pattern than we took it at first to be. The baby, let us say, starts with the theory that the combination of a certain colour of complexion with the human form is part of the world-pattern ; he supposes, on the basis of experience, that all men are white. Then he is shown by his nurse a picture of black men. This conflicts with his reason in the same sense in which the statement that a man rose from the dead conflicts with our reason ; that is to say, it conflicts with his experience. Two alternatives are before the child. Either (1) there is not a pattern at all, the universe is irrational, or (2) the theory he had formed of the pattern must be corrected. Having reason deep in his mental constitution, the child instinctively chooses the latter. And he can amend his theory of the pattern in two ways. The trouble, remember, is that two uniformities he had observed in his experience conflict if they are both extended as universal laws of the pattern beyond his experience. One uniformity is that what his nurse has hitherto told him has turned out to be true, the other is that men are white. Either therefore the simple law, My nanny speaks the truth, must be replaced by the more complicated law, My nanny speaks the truth only in certain circumstances, or the simple law, All men are white, must be replaced by the more complicated law, Men are white or black according to circumstances. The child holds as firmly as ever to the essential faith of reason : " There is a pattern " ; but he has discovered that the pattern is not as simple a one as he had supposed.

Just in this way we can only affirm certainly what events could or could not take place outside the limits of our experience, if we have a complete theory of the pattern of the universe. If it were true to say, The belief that a man rose from the dead is against reason, that could only mean, Any one who asserts that a man rose from the dead, implies thereby that there is no pattern at all ; he denies that the universe is rational. But it is nonsense to say that all those who believe that a man rose from the dead, believe that the universe has no pattern at all. They only hold that the pattern of the universe is more complex than it is held to be by the men who think that the uniformities observed within a certain range of experience are sufficient to give a theory of the whole.

Now it is so obvious that none of us can ever claim to have a complete and final theory of the world-pattern, that all attacks upon the belief in miracles on the ground that they are " against reason " are foolish. Stories of miracles do not conflict with reason ; what they conflict with is a large mass of human experience. This does not prove them to be untrue, because the mass of experience upon which modern natural science is based, although very large, is infinitely smaller than the universe. But it does prevent people accepting the stories of miracles as true, if we can account for these stories existing without being obliged to modify in any particular the theory of the world-pattern which we have hitherto formed on the basis of ordinary common-sense experience. You will remember that when the baby was first told about black men, he had the alternatives of adjusting his theory of the universe to the new fact, either by supposing that black men really existed or by supposing that his nurse was not speaking the truth. Similarly here we have the datum : certain human witnesses declare that such and such miraculous events took place. We can deal with this fact either by supposing that the witnesses do not give a true account, or by supposing that the pattern of the universe is really such as to include events of that kind. Now it seems to a large number of people to-day that the first way of dealing with these stories is much simpler than the second.

The real attack upon miraculous stories to-day is not made by metaphysics or by physical science, whose theories are so plainly imperfect and provisional that they cannot possibly claim to give a final and complete theory of the world-pattern. The real attack is made by psychology and anthropology. For these sciences claim to show how naturally the stories would arise under certain individual and social conditions of mind, even if the events they allege never took place. They do not attempt to prove that the events *could not* have taken place ; all they purport to do is to take the value out of the testimony that they did take place.

This state of the case is ignored both by those people who go on talking against the belief in miracles on the ground that they are " against reason," and by Christian apologists who take great pains to prove that there is no valid metaphysical or scientific reason why such events should not take place. This is to defend a position at a point where the repulse of an attack is easy, after the real attack has shifted to another quarter. The question is : Are these stories more easily accounted for by the hypothesis that they are true or by the hypothesis that they were due to deception or mistake ? It is possible to conceive testimony so strong that it would be reasonable to accept it, even if it involved our adopting a theory of the world-pattern which we should never have formed on the basis of our personal experience alone and the personal experience of all living people known to us. Is the testimony supporting any miraculous story of this strength ? In spite of the explanations offered by modern psychology and anthropology, there are still people who answer this question, in the case of some miraculous stories, by Yes. But there are two different accounts given of this strength of the testimony, and we must carefully distinguish them. According to one account the testimony is strong because, if we take it just as human testimony and apply the common-sense rules of evidence to it, it is convincing in spite of the exceptional character of the event alleged. That is to say, to suppose the testimony false would involve a worse disturbance of our present theory of the world-pattern, because it would imply such a departure from all our present ideas of human psychology, than the disturbance involved in the supposition that the event alleged really took place. To take, for instance, the narrative of Christ's rising from the dead. It is easier, this argument says, to suppose that His dead body really was re-animated than to suppose that the account in our documents rests upon illusion or fraud. It was on this ground presumably that Seeley, in " Ecce Homo," referred to the Resurrection of Christ as an event for which there was convincing historical evidence. Seeley spoke as a historian, not as a Christian, for his own theory of the universe seems to have differed materially from the Christian one. The other account given of the strength of the testimony is that it is strong because it is divinely inspired.

Reason and Dogma

Whether it is strong or not, as judged by the ordinary rules of human evidence, you must accept it because it is given on the authority of God Himself, speaking through the Bible or through the Church ; you must accept it by faith.

Well, with regard to the first argument, is it true that the testimony to such miracles as the resurrection of the body of Christ or His walking upon the water or His multiplication of the loaves is so strong, just as human testimony, that to accept them as having really happened is the easiest hypothesis ? Personally I cannot see that it is. If you took, for example, the narratives of Christ's Resurrection just as the Society for Psychical Research takes documents submitted to it, I cannot think that they would appear first-class documents. In the first place there are the obvious discrepancies between the different accounts ; in the second place, there is the impossibility of putting further questions to the witnesses. Both these things would be serious detractions from the value of the testimony from the point of view of the Society for Psychical Research. And even if you ultimately inclined upon the basis of the documents to accept the fact alleged as true, all you would have got would be a balance of probabilities ; you could never verify your conclusion. But you can hardly take as a basic fact in your religion something which you regard as on the whole rather more likely to have happened than not.

Yet while we admit that the truth of these events can never be satisfactorily established on a simple balance of probabilities, we must recognize, I think, that there is no such clear balance of probability *against* them as " Rationalists " would make out. For remember the " Rationalist " contention is : Because in the limited field of experience which we can verify, we never find events of this kind, therefore the probability against such events ever having occurred is overwhelming. But the theory of those who believe in them, is not that they are ordinary events ; they are not events which, on this theory, *would* occur in normal human experience. The fact therefore that they are not found in ordinary experience can hardly be urged against the theory ; there is no reason why they should be found. Take the story of Christ's walking on the water. Supposing it is true that some spiritual or psychic power exists which under certain rare and peculiar conditions counteracts the force of gravitation, the data before us to-day are just the data we should on that supposition expect to find. We should expect, that is, to find occasional testimony to such events having taken place in the case of some extraordinary personalities, and we should expect such testimony to be rare and very difficult to verify. We have, remember, the alleged phenomenon of " levitation," which seems to have a certain body of testimony in favour of its having occurred at various times and in various parts of the world. It is difficult to say that probability is either against or for these stories, because the conditions under which they are stated to have occurred are not conditions we can reconstruct at will, and the negative result of ordinary experience cannot therefore be urged against them.

The only way, it seems to me, in which the stories of miraculous events in the past can receive decisive confirmation, is by manifestation of the same, or a similar, power in immediate experience ; apart from that, no argument as to probabilities takes us much farther. Supposing you could have in our own day some thoroughly verified case of levitation, the story of Christ's walking on the water would receive an immense accession of probability. There are Christians who believe that the same spiritual power which operated in an extraordinary way upon the material world in the case of Christ and some of the saints in former times ought to be permanently resident in the Church, if the Church was as it should be. We have in these stories instances of a spiritual power which men of faith ought to exert to-day. If that is so, the historical truth of these stories is important. If on the other hand we believe that the power of working what are called " miracles " has long ago ceased, then I do not see that it is of any practical consequence whether the old stories are true or not. Supposing the stories of Christ's stilling the storm and feeding the multitude *were* true, they could in that case be of edification to us to-day simply as figures of what we may expect Christ to do here and now—that is, still our inward spiritual conflicts and feed us with spiritual food. But, as figures, the stories would serve their purpose equally well whether they were literally true or not.

Those who say that the truth of the miracles in question must be accepted by faith, hold so far a stronger position than those who base belief in them on a calculation of probabilities. A very large amount of our beliefs about the world we hold by trust in the testimony of particular persons. If we have reason to believe that the authority in a certain case is trustworthy, unquestionably to accept it is the most rational thing to do.

Hellenism and Christianity

The critical question here is : What justification is there for the initial act of faith ? What is its relation to reason ?

No doubt we must recognize that at the basis of all religion there is an act of faith. So, in a sense, there is at the basis of all rationalist theory with regard to things we have not directly experienced. In both cases we make a leap from our immediate experience, from the fragment of the world-pattern we have seen, to a belief in what is there beyond the field of our vision. In rationalist inference we make the leap in the trust that laws or uniformities we have discovered in the little bit of the pattern we have seen hold good over all the rest. You can never prove that the universe is rational, because all such argument would be a begging of the question to start with. Our belief that the universe is rational, the pre-supposition of all rationalism, is itself an act of faith.

At the basis of religion is another act of faith : the belief that the universe is rational in another sense— in the sense in which we describe an action as rational when it has a reasonable end, when it is worth doing. The faith of religion is that the good we discover or know in the human spirit is that for which the universe exists. If, for instance, spirit, and all the good and beauty it recognizes, came in the process of time to an utter end with the extinction of life on the planet, the world would be without meaning. If the world is to have a meaning, the spirit tells us that certain things *ought to be ;* the faith of religion is that they *are.* The belief in the coincidence of what *ought to be* with what *is* is the religious act of faith : you cannot prove it ; neither can you disprove it.

Reason and Dogma

Why should we make any leap at all, why not confine ourselves to the little bit of reality we have seen ? The answer is that we are not only spectators of reality, we are also makers of reality. When we *act*, we create a new bit of reality. If we were merely spectators—minds suspended in space looking on inactive at the world-process—we might, so far as I can see, be purely agnostic. We might abstain from making any guess as to the part of the pattern, if pattern there is, not yet disclosed to us, and simply wait and see what happened. But we are under the necessity of doing something in the world, of making our own new contribution to reality. Even if we resolved to sit absolutely still till we died, if we did die (for if we are purely agnostic we must not affirm that death will necessarily be the consequence of abstinence from food), that would be a sort of conduct chosen by an act of will. The movement of time compels us, whether we want to or not, to act. But for action we need to form some hypothesis as to the universe in which we act, as to what lies beyond the range of previous experience. It is before the compulsion to act that all pure agnosticism breaks down.

The religious man bases his action on the hypothesis that the universe is such as to realize in the long run the good which is revealed to him in the human spirit, that spirit, and not matter, is the really dominant thing in the universe. His faith is an act of trust in the universe, and, if he is convinced, as most religious men are, that without God the good he recognizes could not be realized, that life could not have a meaning, then his act of trust in the universe may be also called an act of trust in God. He chooses this hypothesis, not because it is the only one

which is logically possible on the data before him, but
because it appears to him, as a spiritual being, the worthiest
of all possible hypotheses to live by. Our faith is not
what we are prepared to demonstrate by argument, but
what we are prepared to live by and die for : the typical
assertor of Christianity is the martyr. And if the Christian belief is true that ultimately God will ask an account
of each individual's faith, He will not ask how much we
were able to prove, but what we determined to make the
real principle of our action.

If we adopted a hypothesis as to the universe logically
irreconcilable with the little bit we see, our choice would,
I think, be justly described as irrational. But the religious
hypothesis is neither proved nor disproved by our limited
experience. We are compelled, as we have seen, to make
a leap of some sort beyond our experience, and we choose
to leap in that direction rather than in another. There
are a number of hypotheses all equally compatible in pure
logic with the bit of the world-pattern we have seen.
The bit of the universe, consider, shown us by our experience consists in great part of the uniformities of the
material world, the movements of material mass, which
seem to have no spiritual or moral purpose, but it also
includes the human spirit in all its various manifestations,
culminating in Him, the Son of Man. Now it seems to
me we can, without being illogical, choose either element
in our experience to interpret the whole by. We may
choose to take the brute material mass with its uniformities as the key to reality, and explain the phenomena of
the human spirit simply as a chance and ephemeral
outcome of material laws. Or we may take the human
spirit as the key, and regard the material world as

ultimately there to subserve a spiritual end. I do not see why even such an hypothesis as that the ultimate Reality behind the universe was a malignant and not a good power should not be possible in pure logic. All the appearances of good and of human value in the world we might explain as contributing to produce in the end a greater volume of evil and misery than could be produced without them. The religious man chooses to take the good and the beauty revealed in the human spirit at its highest and best as giving the real purport and meaning of the Whole.

No doubt this trust in the religious man does not appear to him an hypothesis arbitrarily chosen, but a conviction held with deep personal certitude. Often, as life goes on, its events serve to make this certitude deeper and greater. An analogy, I think, is the certain trust which a man feels in his friend. He believes in his friend's goodwill, although that goodwill is not manifested in every part of his friend's behaviour. There are large tracts of his friend's behaviour which are neutral in character, numberless actions he does mechanically by simple habit, walking, eating, sleeping. Other parts of his conduct may even bear the appearance of disloyalty or ill-will. But there have been moments of intense self-revelation, moments when his eyes have looked into the eyes of his friend and the two human souls have touched and known each other, and for ever after those are the moments which he takes as the key to all his friend's conduct ; there the spirit was disclosed which gives it all its purport and meaning. Behind the mechanical actions which by themselves tell nothing of the friend's personality, he knows that the personality

Hellenism and Christianity

is still there. Even when there is the appearance of ill-will, he trusts still; he is sure that ultimately his friend's conduct in this particular will be explained and be found consistent with faithful love.

So Christians believe that the inner Reality of the universe has looked into human eyes through the eyes of Jesus Christ, and behind all the appearances of indifference and heartlessness in the material tracts of the world, for them He is always there. The universe in its totality will ultimately be found to be the best possible embodiment and manifestation of the Divine Will and Wisdom and Love.

Now you might point out to the man who trusted his friend in the way described that his hypothesis as to his friend's personality was an arbitrary one. He was not logically compelled to take those particular moments in his intercourse with his friend as the key to the whole; he might equally have chosen the times when his friend seemed indifferent as showing him as he really was, and he might have construed the occasional appearance of love by the indifferent moments and not the seemingly indifferent moments by the occasional appearance of love. There is an element of deliberate will in his choosing the hypothesis he does. But he feels that he could do no otherwise without violating what in himself is best. I do not mean that in all cases it is wise to place this trust, in spite of appearances, in another man. Sometimes people trust foolishly. It depends on the quality of those moments of mutual communication how far it is right to build this trust upon them. But there are cases when I may feel rightly that the evidence a man has given me of trustworthiness at certain moments,

242

warrants me in trusting the man—one might almost say absolutely. We may always be deceived. So may those who determine to trust the universe because of those manifestations in humanity be deceived. We ought frankly to admit this; we take the risks of trusting. Yet in the case of a man's trust in his friend, this admission of the theoretical possibility of his being deceived does not affect his inner feeling of certainty, his " moral certainty," as we say. It is not the same sort of certainty as the certainty induced by logical compulsion, but in its intensity and force as a psychological factor it is just as great as logical certainty. And if the hypothesis that the inner reality of the universe is revealed in good men and especially in Christ, cannot be logically proved, neither can any of the other hypotheses about the universe—that it has no moral quality, that it is indifferent to good and evil, that it is essentially unknowable —be proved. In its character of a leap beyond experience the hypothesis of the Christian believer is no worse off than any of those other hypotheses; all are leaps beyond experience. A leap of some kind we are compelled to make by the necessity of action. The Christian believer chooses this hypothesis, because he chooses to accept the scale of spiritual values given him in his moral and mental constitution as veridical.

So far we have shown how the hypothesis of the Christian believer is faith, but we have not yet shown how it can be the acceptance of any authority embodied in other human beings. This, however, is what we have to do, if miracles are to be accepted in any sense as facts on the authority of the Church or the writers of the Bible. To go then a step further, we may, I think, see that the spiritual values which a man now recognizes by his own inner light, he did not originally discover all by himself. We do not know how much of them would have ever entered his consciousness, if he had grown up in isolation in a desert island. He discovered them because they were already expressed in the tradition of some society or community with which he came into contact after his entrance into the world. He did not accept them blindly, without any confirmation in his own spirit ; he has come, he says, to see for himself that the ideals embodied in this society are higher than any other he can conceive. (It is very analogous to the training of the artist ; his ideals are formed under the influence of art-traditions existing before him, but when they have been formed they are his own personal conviction.) Just as it is reasonable for a man to say, I see in Christ the most perfect manifestation I can conceive of Spirit, and therefore take Christ as the most perfect manifestation of the inner reality of the universe ; so if a man finds that the tradition of a particular society or community or church gives him a view of the universe which satisfies better than any other the exigencies of his spiritual and moral nature, and that it also produces in the life of its members the spiritual fruits which seem to him the highest in value, it seems reasonable that he should take this view as his working hypothesis as to the constitution of the universe. But here we come upon a difficulty. The theory we have just stated seems all right as long as what we have to do with are either values, e.g. the doctrine that the best thing in the world is love, or suppositions about the universe which are essential if reality is to correspond to value, e.g. the doctrine that God *is* love ; for in both these cases the tradition can be confirmed by the man's own personal spirit. He can see for himself that the tradition of a community speaks the truth when it affirms that love is the best thing in the world, and that, if reality is to correspond to value, the inner reality of the universe, God, must be love. In neither of these cases therefore does the man accept the traditional teaching blindly, without the confirmation of his own inner sense. But it is quite different where it is a question of concrete events in history, of particular miracles. Can any inner spiritual sense give information to a man as to whether Christ really did walk on the water or feed five thousand with five loaves ?

I do not think we could attach much value to such an argument as : Because this community speaks the truth on questions of spiritual value, therefore I ought to accept its authority on matters of fact. Authority is essentially relative to particular fields. A man who speaks with authority on art, does not necessarily speak with authority on strategical problems. The Catholic theory itself limits the authority of the Church to questions *de fide et moribus*, questions concerned with faith and morals. Only it includes under the term " faith " belief as to a large number of alleged historical events. A man must believe that events of which he can get no verification in experience took place because the Church says they did. Now in the field of spiritual values it seems to me that a man may reasonably respect the authority of a community on a particular point, even where his own judgement does not confirm it, so long as his judgement does confirm on a large number of other points the view of that community. For instance, a

Hellenism and Christianity

man who found that the Christian view of life as a whole satisfied him and that Christianity showed a power of producing in practice the richest virtues, might reasonably say : " I do not see for myself that suicide or polygamy is wrong, but since the Christian tradition emphatically condemns these things, I think it is probable that my own moral judgement is here defective and that suicide or polygamy really is wrong." Just as a judge of art might say : " I do not see for myself that this work is good, but, since it is universally admired by the people whose judgement I have learned to respect, I think that probably my own artistic sense is here defective." And he might reasonably act on this hypothesis, if he were commissioned, let us say, to buy pictures for a public gallery. It is reasonable in certain cases for a man to subordinate his own judgement to authority. But these are cases where the field in which he trusts the authority, unconfirmed by his own judgement, is the *same* field in which the teaching of the authority has been as a whole confirmed by his judgement. If on the other hand you say : " I trust the Church as to matters of historical fact, because my own judgement confirms the Church's teaching as to spiritual values," you are passing to a wholly different field, and the procedure does not appear to me reasonable.

The only matters of fact, it seems to me, as to which the Church can claim respect for its authority, are those which are essential, if reality is to correspond to value —if the *is* coincides ultimately with the *ought to be*. For instance, to a Christian it seems plain that, if the universe is really such as to satisfy the demands of the spirit, God must be, and must be of the character attributed to Him

Reason and Dogma

in the Christian faith. Here therefore the Christian Church teaches with authority when it makes an affirmation as to what is. But are the miraculous events in the Gospels in the same way facts essential to the Christian view of the universe, things which must actually have occurred, if reality corresponds to the Christian scheme of values?

In regard to such alleged miracles as the walking upon the water, the feeding of the five thousand, the changing of water into wine, it is hard to see how we can answer this question by Yes. It is hard to see how it makes any difference to the Christian faith as to the character of God and the Person of Jesus Christ whether these particular narratives are historical fact or mythology. With regard to them, I think, the only considerations which apply are those which estimate the probability or improbability of the stories in the light of experience. When we come to the two great miracles associated with the Person of Christ, the Virgin Birth and the Resurrection, the case is much more problematic. No doubt the Christian doctrine of the Person of Christ does profoundly affect the Christian view of God. If it can be shown that the Christian doctrine of the Person of Christ essentially requires that Christ should have been born of a virgin, that Christ could not be God in the sense required by Christian theology if He had a human father as well as a human mother, then the belief in the Virgin Birth would no doubt be part of the Christian belief about God, and the Virgin Birth would be one of those things which must be presupposed, if the universe is to correspond with the Christian scheme of values. Personally, I do not see that this has ever been shown. I do not see that the Christian belief as to the Person of Christ depends at all upon the truth of this story ; and if it does not, the story becomes simply one which there is neither any good ground for affirming, because the evidence for it is very doubtful, nor good ground for denying, because the case is so obviously unique that probability and improbability cannot here be estimated by our ordinary experience.

The other great miracle associated with the Person of Christ is the Resurrection. Here I think we must distinguish between the Resurrection in the sense of the continued activity of Christ after His death, in the full reality and power of His personal life, and the reanimation of His dead body. The Resurrection in the first sense *is* essential to the Christian faith. The experience of the disciples after the Crucifixion, those appearances which convinced them that Jesus was alive, can have been no subjective illusion ; they must have been a real manifestation of Himself by the living Christ. But the truth of this does not seem to me to depend on whether the body taken down from the Cross was reanimated or not. The story of the empty tomb would, on such a view, be another of the stories which the evidence, combined with our experience, gives us no warrant either to affirm or to deny.

XIII

CHRISTIANITY IN THE MODERN WORLD

WHETHER the faith of the Christian Church be based upon reality or be a mere delusion, there can be no question as to the continued existence of Christianity as a fact in the world. Of the individuals composing the human race at this moment of time conventionally described as A.D. 1921, many millions still profess to hold Christian beliefs. Of these millions a certain proportion really do hold Christian beliefs. Neither the people therefore whose aim is to make all the world Christian, nor the people whose aim is to eradicate Christianity from the earth, can claim that their efforts have so far reached consummation. The verdict of history has not yet been pronounced : Christianity has neither won the whole of mankind, nor gone as yet the way of the ancient religions of Egypt and Babylon. The present state of things is felt both by Christians and by the opponents of Christianity to be transitional. Transitional to what ? That is the question.

We answer that question largely in accordance with our convictions as to what is abstractly true. It is hard for a man to believe that the strength of his convictions is not an objective force before which contrary beliefs

Hellenism and Christianity

in other people must go down like ninepins. A predicter naturally assumes the old maxim that Truth is great and will prevail—an assumption which a Christian must logically expect to be justified in the long run, though it entails a somewhat questionable act of faith on the part of an Agnostic or " Rationalist." [1] Is mankind, the by-product of a haphazard world, necessarily determined in the direction of truth rather than of pleasant or profitable error ? There are, indeed, among those who repudiate Christianity men of an aristocratic cast of mind, who would scorn to desire any confirmation for their case from popular success. Anything like counting heads seems to them an irrelevant, and even vicious, procedure in questions which ought to be settled by pure reason. Such men would readily admit that Christianity may be on the eve of some fresh triumphs without thinking any the better of it for that. And one must surely allow that for every honest person the question " Is Christianity true or false ? " is a more important question than " Is Christianity a winning or a losing cause ? " Yet to whichever camp one belongs, this latter question has a quasi-historical interest ; and even if it is unworthy of a reasonable being to make his own beliefs depend upon

[1] Rationalism, in its proper sense of the organization of the matter of experience by the reason, was spoken of in the first essay as the characteristic mark of modern Western civilization. In that sense every reasonable man, whether a Christian or not a Christian, is a Rationalist. Since, however, a large number of the opponents of Christianity to-day call themselves Rationalists, as if they were reasonable in an altogether special way, I refer to them under that name in this essay. It seems generally preferable to describe any set of people by the name they themselves affect (as when one speaks of the " Orthodox " Church) ; that does not, of course, imply that one acknowledges the name to be appropriate in fact.

the suffrage of the crowd, we should be inhuman if we did not care how a cause which we held true prospered among our fellow-men.

This huge complicated world, the sum of countless interacting tendencies, a web of millions of individual purposes, driven by forces that are often dark till they issue in apparently abrupt explosions—incalculable, changeful, exhaustless—which of us can see more than a little way into its working?

What each man sees, when he attempts to read the signs of his own time, will no doubt depend largely upon what things he has chanced to encounter, and the peculiar angle from which he observes. If, however, he gives a candid report of what he sees, that may have its value as one personal contribution to be added to the volume of testimony.

One patent fact confronting every observer is that the division between Christians and non-Christians is not peculiar to any class or social grade or level of culture, but exists everywhere and at all levels.

If we viewed modern civilization under the image of a mountain like Dante's Purgatory, with the different levels representing degrees of education and knowledge, we should see the division between Christians and non-Christians, not as a horizontal one, dividing off a higher part of the mountain from the part below, but as a vertical one running through the mountain from top to base. On the very highest level, among those who lead the advance, as the original workers and thinkers, in the various departments of knowledge and thought, Christians and opponents of Christianity are found side by side; at the bottom, among the most ignorant and uncultured,

there are those who seem to themselves to have come
into touch with the great Reality in Christianity, and
those for whom all that order of things is without meaning.
This state of things may seem at first sight to be equally
favourable and equally unfavourable to the claims of
Christianity and to those of " Rationalism." It is really
more unfavourable to the " Rationalist," and for a plain
reason. Christians do not assert that their belief is
arrived at as a scientific inference from universally
recognized data, in such wise that a man has only to
be learned enough in order to be shut up to the Christian
conclusion. If among the data which determine the
belief are certain special experiences of the inner life,
certain special perceptions of value, which come independently of the particular individual's amount of knowledge
and culture, then there is no difficulty in understanding
that the division between Christians and non-Christians
should appear at all levels. The " Rationalist," on the
other hand, does claim that his objection to Christianity
is based upon scientific knowledge ; he does claim that
a man has only to be learned enough in order to be
logically bound to deny the truth of Christianity ; for
him, therefore, it is a really awkward fact that Christianity
should find adherents among people at the top level.
According to his theory it is intellectual enlightenment
which causes the decay of Christianity ; if so, we should
see its withering away begin from the top of the mountain. There it is to-day, flourishing at the very highest
level. What hope, then, is there of its speedy extinction
lower down ?

There are various ways in which the " Rationalist "
can deal with this phenomenon. One is to pretend that

Christianity in the Modern World

it does not exist, to talk as if no educated person were a Christian, or could be a Christian. This is the way of bluff; but it is felt by all the more candid and serious opponents of Christianity to be unworthy, and is only successful in any marked degree with the credulous and the young. Loyally recognizing the facts, the " Rationalist " may try to explain them in a way which leaves his position undamaged. He may, for instance, urge the extent to which unreason and obstinacy vitiate human judgement; even when a man is learned enough to have all the proper data before him, sentiments and desires, especially those bred in him by associations of his childhood and the prevalent tradition, may enter in to corrupt the process of inference; *amour propre* may lead him to cling to an opinion to which he is once committed. The Archbishop of Canterbury, for instance, could not announce that he had been brought over to the views of Mr. Joseph McCabe without some sacrifice of dignity. All this is abundantly true: and if the anti-Christian has first persuaded us of the truth of his beliefs, we shall naturally have to explain by such psychological causes the fact that so many persons of great knowledge and discretion do not accept them. So long, however, as the " Rationalist " contention does not seem to us cogent, we shall reflect that it is not Christians only whose judgements are apt to be vitiated by personal prejudice. One cannot imagine that it would be exactly easy for Mr. McCabe to announce that he had been brought over to the views of the Archbishop of Canterbury. Considering the large play which irrational feelings have in all of us, modesty and self-examination come amiss to no one, whatever opinion he may stand for; and it may perhaps temper our confidence, when we are ready by some facile psychological explanation to dispose of the opinion held by people equally well informed with ourselves, to remember that they in all probability have taken our explanation into account, when they analysed the grounds of their own belief and tried to make allowance for those disturbing factors. Do we really suppose that any intelligent Christian has not been aware of something so obvious as the power of childish association or the influence of environment and not asked himself repeatedly how far such things have entered illegitimately into the formation of his personal beliefs ? I should feel it unfair to deny that an intelligent " Rationalist " might occasionally feel a doubt shoot through his mind : " Supposing, after all, Christians should have got nearer the Truth than I have ! "

There is another line which a " Rationalist " may take. He may point out that when he affirms an incompatibility between Christianity and Science he does not mean that a conflict takes place in every single department of knowledge. It is only on the field of particular sciences that conflict arises. If, however, the well-established results of inquiry in any field are irreconcilable with Christian belief, that is enough to disprove it logically : it will be no use for the Christian to plead that in other fields of knowledge there is no collision. If a single hole be knocked in a ship, it is poor comfort to point out that the rest of the frame is unaffected. And if an irreconcilable conflict occurs in any field, the ordinary " educated " man, who possesses, it is supposed, a general acquaintance with the results of the particular sciences, takes note that Christianity has been doomed. On the other hand,

Christianity in the Modern World

a man may attain great distinction along limited lines of inquiry, may attain vast special knowledge, without having sufficient general information to be aware of the conflict.

The people we have spoken of as being at the top of the mountain may consist largely of men eminent indeed for their learning or scientific knowledge, but not learned just in those fields which matter. The Christian is therefore wide of the mark when he points to this or to that distinguished name and asks whether So-and-so is not both a *savant* and a believer. The "Rationalist" will want to know in what direction his learning lies. He would have no difficulty in admitting that a man might be the European authority on beetles or Byzantine Greek, and at the same time a devout Christian.

Perhaps the fact is not enough recognized either on the Christian or the anti-Christian side. The objections brought against Christian belief are drawn from some few of the many fields of knowledge ; in the great majority of fields there is no conflict, because there is no contact. And what exactly, we may ask ourselves, are those fields in which conflict is alleged to-day ? There is a common notion that it is principally in fields which belong to the category of Natural Science. This, I believe, is altogether a mistake. Such conflicts were, no doubt, prominent in the past generation. Scientific Geology was irreconcilable with the old Hebrew cosmogonies : Biology left no place for the Garden of Eden.

Now however that the great mass of educated Christian opinion has come to recognize the mythological character of the book of Genesis, and has adjusted itself to theories of Evolution, there is no longer any collision on those fields. I believe that there is no conflict anywhere in what is ordinarily known as Natural Science ; those who speak of such a conflict are repeating old phrases without regard to the changes which have made them no longer true.

The fields in which Christianity has to contend to-day are those of Anthropology, Philosophy, and Experimental Psychology.

The modern science of Anthropology has involved the comparative study of religions, and this, as conducted by certain of its prominent exponents, has tended to assimilate Christianity to the other forms of religion which have prevailed in the world, and to represent all religion as the mere survival of childish superstition. It is no longer possible to regard the Christian religion as something absolutely different from the rest, and the line between religion and superstition has certainly become much harder to draw. A special inquiry of crucial importance in this field has been that into the origins of Christianity. Close links have been shown between primitive Christianity and the cults or mysteries which were being propagated at that epoch in the Mediter-ranean world, and theories are current according to which a great part of Christianity was simply pagan mystery-religion taken over bodily. An extreme view along these lines is one which denies even the historical existence of Jesus Christ—a view which, one must admit, has not managed to establish itself among the educated, outside a little circle of amateurs and cranks, or to rise above the dignity of the Baconian theory of Shakespeare.[1]

[1] " The doubts which have been cast on the historical reality of Jesus are in my judgement unworthy of serious attention. Quite

Christianity in the Modern World

All such theories, we note at this point, belong to the province of the anthropologist.

It is in the field of Philosophy that the intellectual issues between Christianity and its opponents are to-day really centred.

The anthropological attack can at the most do no more than create a presumption against Christianity's unique claims ; if it can draw Christianity into the general process of religious change and trace the history of its beliefs and practices, the further question, what real value underlie the historical process, it is no longer for Anthropology to answer. That belongs to Philosophy. The difficulties, again, which are supposed to beset Christianity from the standpoint of Natural Science belong not to Natural Science, but to Philosophy. In one form or another these difficulties are all varieties of a single objection—the objection of the " Rationalist " to recognize as a force in the Universe anything in the nature of rational Will, anything whose operations might interfere with the rigidly fixed sequence by which one material state of the Universe succeeds another, according to laws out of relation to any Purpose or End. In its extreme form of Materialism, the objection denies that anything exists in the Universe, except matter governed by the purposeless invariable laws. Materialism is not a doctrine of

apart from the positive evidence of history and tradition, the origin of a great religious and moral reform is inexplicable without the personal existence of a great reformer. To dissolve the founder of Christianity into a myth, as some would do, is hardly less absurd than it would be to do the same for Mohammed, Luther, and Calvin. Such dissolving views are for the most part the dreams of students who know the great world chiefly through its pale reflection in books."—Sir James Frazer, " The Golden Bough," Part VI (" The Scapegoat "), p. 412.

Hellenism and Christianity

Natural Science. Physics may show the operation of certain laws governing matter, when left to itself, but Physics cannot assert that there is no Reality besides. That is a *philosophical* hypothesis. It may be true or false, but Science can no more prove it experimentally than Dr. Johnson could disprove Berkeley's Idealism by kicking a large stone. Materialism in its crude form is discredited to-day with the educated class in England, but views are still prevalent which amount to very much the same thing. The difficulty, of course, confronting all such theories at the outset is the plain existence of human and animal volition ; something which seems, at any rate, to interfere with the mechanical processes in a sufficiently incalculable way. Extreme Materialism affirmed that Mind was really only a form of Matter ; this is now generally perceived to have been nonsense. But the spirit of Materialism is preserved in the theories which go under the names of Epiphenomenalism or Parallelism, theories which recognize the existence of Mind, as something different from Matter, but deny it any power of deflecting or influencing in the slightest degree the processes of matter. The action of every living creature would, according to this theory, be calculable if we only knew enough, as the result of purely material, purposeless laws, the chance impact of molecule on molecule in the brain producing movements in the nerves and muscles, quite independently of the Consciousness which accompanies the process as an idle shadow.

If it is only as such a shadow or accompaniment of material processes that Consciousness can exist, or if, existing independently of the material world, it is otiose, then certainly the Christian belief as to God and the Soul

Christianity in the Modern World

are delusions. Here we have only to note that all these theories are not the results of experimental Science, but metaphysical hypotheses, whose worth it belongs to Philosophy to determine. All that has been said finds special illustration in reference to what is often supposed to be the great quarrel of Science with Christianity—the question of miracles. It is supposed that " Science " shows miracles to be impossible. It is alleged, for instance, that one rose from the dead. What can Biology say to disprove it ? Nothing, except that in the field of its experience it has discovered no agency capable of making life return to a dead body. But there is no reason why it should, on the hypothesis of those who believe in the miracle : their whole contention is that the event was determined by a volition of an altogether exceptional kind. Biology can only speak for the field which it knows : it cannot pretend to give an exhaustive statement of all the agencies existing in the Universe. And so with all the other Natural Sciences. Each can exhibit the laws which under normal circumstances govern its subject-matter, but before the allegation of any exceptional and irruptive cause they are dumb. The objections to the story that one rose from the dead are not drawn from Natural Science, but from Philosophy and from Anthropology.

From Philosophy, because the proposition " No agency exists *in the Universe* capable of making life return to a dead body " is a philosophical proposition. Or, again, the objection is sometimes put in the way that miracles violate the " Uniformity of Nature." If by the Uniformity of Nature is meant the doctrine that similar effects invariably follow from similar causes, miracles, so far from violating it, presuppose it, since, *ex hypothesi*, an exceptional volition enters as a cause into the conditions of the particular case ; miracles can be declared to violate the Uniformity of Nature only on the supposition that we have already discovered enough about Nature to say definitely that certain things are impossible in any circumstances. This supposition is a question for Philosophy.

Probably, however, the philosophical and *a priori* objections to miracles are not those which weigh most at the present time. It is rather Anthropology than Philosophy which makes men incredulous when confronted with the story of a resurrection. The real difficulty lies in the great number of miraculous stories which are admittedly untrue. The anthropologist is dealing with them perpetually in his ordinary day's work. He expects them as a natural product on certain levels of culture or under certain intellectual conditions. He accustoms himself to estimate the testimony by which they are supported in a way which allows for the immense scope of imagination, invention, and credulity. It is difficult for him, when he comes to the miracles of the Christian story, suddenly to apply new canons, to regard them as something wholly different from those with which he is familiar elsewhere. Even if it could be shown by abstract metaphysical reasoning that there was nothing inherently impossible in a miracle, that would produce little effect upon the hardened anthropologist. His business is simply to estimate the evidential value of the documents produced in each particular case, regard being had to what his studies have taught him of the working of the human mind.

Christianity in the Modern World

The question of miracles is perhaps not central to Christianity. If one is convinced, for instance, that the evidence for the reanimation of the body of Christ s insufficient, it seems still possible to believe in Christ as a living Person. But so far as the question of miracles exercises men's minds to-day, it is important, I think, to realize that the difficulty is not made by Natural Science, nor even mainly by Philosophy, but by Anthropology.

The field of Philosophy has itself many subdivisions. We have so far considered only the metaphysical department, on which, as we have seen, Christianity is confronted with theories running counter to its central beliefs concerning God and the Soul, and by theories running counter to its more peripheral belief in miracles. But it is not only in the metaphysical department that conflict arises. In that of Epistemology, Christianity meets theories which deny the validity of the mental processes involved in Christian faith. Christianity certainly involves beliefs about existences transcending the phenomenal world. Are such beliefs ever legitimate for the human mind ? Agnosticism says No, and Agnosticism is an epistemological theory. We have again believers in an Inner Light, a super-intellectual irradiation, and people who deny that the experience pointed to is any road to real knowledge. Do the convictions involved in religious faith purport even to be knowledge, or is there a religious knowledge of a different order from scientific knowledge ? All such controversies, in which Christianity is necessarily engaged, belong to the field of epistemological thought.

Another department of Philosophy is the Ethical : and in this, too, Christianity has a conflict to sustain.

The values which it affirms are challenged. It posits certain relations between God and Man, which are declared in some quarters to be immoral, by those, for instance, who maintain that the idea of forgiveness implies an illegitimate interference with the chain of moral consequences ; or they are declared to be unworthy as, for instance, by Mr. Lowes Dickinson, who finds the idea of love existing between God and a human soul ridiculous and repulsive. Christianity, again, posits certain relations between men and men, and it is against these, described by such names as slave-morality, that writers like Nietzsche have directed the brunt of their attack. Or, thirdly, the Christian view of a man's relations to himself is challenged. Self-control is derided in the name of the principle of Self-realization. In all these controversies we are not concerned with facts which can be scientifically determined, but with spiritual or moral values, where assertion butts against assertion, and individual perception alone for each man can decide. So far as there is any room for argument, there is room for systematic thought, and systematic thought in this field is called Moral Philosophy.

We come to the last field of inquiry in which to-day Christianity is concerned to defend itself : the field on the confines, as it were, between Philosophy and Natural Science, that of Experimental or Descriptive Psychology. A great deal has been written, especially in America, upon the " Psychology of Religion." We cannot say that there is here any direct collision between Christianity and Science. If Psychology describes Christian experience, that leaves still open the question as to its value, and this question is no longer one for Psychology, but for

Christianity in the Modern World

Philosophy in the sense just explained. The study, however, of the Psychology of Religion no doubt may create a certain disposition of mind unfavourable to the Christian claims. Just as the study of Comparative Religion tends to depreciate Christianity by assimilating it to other forms of religion, so the Psychology of Religion may tend to depreciate all religious experience by assimilating it to other, non-religious, forms of experience, and showing its intimate connexion with physiological conditions. Only by a confusion of thought, indeed, can you suppose that you have disposed of Conversion by statistics which show that it normally takes place at the age of puberty, but it is quite true that any one whose mind is immersed in such statistics may find the attitude of the religious man hard to maintain. We may therefore, I think, rightly regard the field of Psychology as one in which Christianity meets opposition to-day.

We have now taken a general survey of the fields where Knowledge and Christianity come into contact, and we have admitted that the attainment of exceptional knowledge on other fields could not be adduced by the Christian apologist to prove that knowledge as a whole was compatible with Christianity. If we found that a man had only to be learned enough as an anthropologist, or eminent enough as a philosopher or psychologist, in order to reject Christianity, we could not get over that fact by adducing eminent chemists or philologists who were Christians. Of course, there is a large educated public which does not consist of specialists in any line ; people who read the weekly reviews, and discuss in club armchairs, and are interested in serious drama—and when one is considering the position of Christianity it might seem more appropriate to take account of the general notions, more or less vague and dilettante, which float amongst this class, than the doctrines of specialists, who are, after all, a much less numerous class of men. The notions of that larger class find expression in the work of the poets and novelists and essay-writers of the day, work which from some points of view may be of a higher order than the books of an academic anthropologist or philosopher. It may be fuller of original thoughts and observations. But there is a difference between all such work, however brilliant, and the work of the specialist in Philosophy. The difference simply is that the philosopher has tried to think systematically about certain problems, while the novelist or essay-writer throws out his thoughts as they come, without feeling bound to co-ordinate them in a logical system. But when we want to know the truth or validity of ideas it is just by ascertaining how they fit into some large system of truth, how they square with other ideas and perceptions, that we can find out. The philosopher is thus working under a control to which writers like Mr. Bernard Shaw or Mr. H. G. Wells, who can fling about their ideas in an easy, free-handed way, are not subject. And when we examine the ideas current amongst the educated on such a subject as Christianity, we find, I think, that they are either fragments caught up from the teaching of professional anthropologists and philosophers, or that, if they are original perceptions, society will not ultimately recognize them as true, unless they can be incorporated in some system by methodical researchers and thinkers. All the criticism of Christianity which one encounters in ordinary conversation will be found to be based upon

Christianity in the Modern World

certain conceptions of anthropology or philosophy or psychology, often casual and fluctuating enough. We are therefore brought round in the end to the question which has hovered before us so long, How is Christianity regarded by the men who stand at the top as authorities in anthropology, philosophy, and psychology ?

And when we look we see that these fields offer no exception to the general fact which we noticed at the outset ; Christians and non-Christians stand side by side. It is plain that knowledge and ability in these fields do not necessarily lead men to Christianity ; for then we should not see the non-Christians. It is equally plain that knowledge and ability in these fields do not make Christian belief impossible ; for then we should not see the Christians. On the hill of knowledge no level has been reached, where a man can say : " Here I am safe ; Christianity cannot touch me here." This state of things is much more awkward for the " Rationalist " than for the Christian.

But there is one substantial part of the " Rationalist's " case which we have not yet heard. " It is all very well," he may say, " to point to a certain number of people who are Christians at this present moment ; but you have overlooked the main point. You are judging of a *movement*, and you cannot take one moment in the process by itself. To know which way things are tending you must look back a little, and see the present moment in its temporal context. A vast change in thought has taken place during the last fifty years, and it is by comparing the Christianity of 1920 with the Christianity of 1870 that we Rationalists can register our success. Not so much that the number of people who openly repudiate Christianity has increased, and that the old social stigma fixed upon the 'infidel' is gone from polite society, but that so great a change has taken place in the inner character of what passes for Christianity to-day. What a different article is covered by the old label! You yourself admit that many of the beliefs we attacked are no longer found on the top level. Which of those anthropologists and philosophers whom you may claim as Christians believes in the truth of everything in the Bible or in the doctrine of everlasting torment? The old orthodoxy at any rate is now met with only at levels a good way down. 'Essays and Reviews' would nowadays not ruffle the surface of the ecclesiastical waters. When we see how Christianity has contracted within its outside shell, we can afford to wait a little longer till it shrivels up altogether and the shell collapses. You have been driven from point to point. Of course, at each retreat you proclaimed that you were not abandoning anything essential. We are afraid that you may have to make the same discovery about many things to which you still cling to-day."

The change indicated by the " Rationalist " is, all intelligent Christians must admit, a very real fact, and a fact which besets them with searching questions. To try to minimize its significance is as unwise on the part of the Christian as it is unwise on the part of the " Rationalist " to try to minimize the significance of the fact that so many people capable of appreciating the change are Christians still. There is, however, one important consideration which the " Rationalist's " argument, as we have stated it, left out. It is not only over the beliefs of the Christian Church that a change has

Christianity in the Modern World

passed during the last two generations. Of the combatants who faced each other fifty years ago none stands the same. If educated Christians have abandoned some of the beliefs of their grandfathers, time has dealt rudely with the fabric of the old Victorian " Rationalism." It is true that the first chapter of Genesis is now esteemed out of date as science, though it continues to have its value as a literary monument. The " Synthetic Philosophy " is also out of date as science ; what value it continues to have as a literary monument it must be left to others to say.

It is not as if a hesitating and hard-driven Christianity were enclosed by a body of opinion, vast, compact, and victorious. There is no doubt some confusion of belief within the Church, but outside of it what we see to-day is Babel. Hundreds start up to bear witness against Chrisʻianity ; the difficulty—as it was of old in the case of the Founder—is to discover two whose witness agrees together. If we sometimes find it a hard problem, What to believe, it is no less haid a problem, What to disbelieve. Supposing that Christianity is not true, does that mean that every single assertion which it implies is untrue ? If no , which assertions are we to reject ? In answer to such a question we can get to-day from the non-Christian world nothing but a babel of voices. I once heard a cynical person compare modern liberal theologians to men sitting in a slowly-heated room, who divested themselves of garment after garment, discussing the while what minimum decency compelled them to keep on. The figure was witty enough, but it seems to me mainly useful by its contrast to the real situation. The whole difficulty of the religious thinker to-day is to know (keeping up the image of the parable) when he has reached nudity. To typify the actual state of things properly we should have to imagine a kind of people who could not easily distinguish their clothes from their skins. While some therefore were keeping on the clothes which they wanted to get rid of, others would be tearing off portions of their skin under the impression they were clothes. That is the religious difficulty to-day.

If there are many, still formally members of a Christian community, who have rejected a mass of beliefs once characteristic of Christians, there are not a few people who stand outside all religious communities and abjure the name of Christian, and who yet have adopted as their personal beliefs large bits of the Christian tradition. It is a question of endless shades and degrees and combinations. There is nothing commoner than to hear people denounce " dogma." What they mean by " dogma " is any belief which they themselves may happen to have discarded. There is a type of Christian who cries aloud that we need to turn from the " dogma of the Churches " to the Living Christ. But belief in the Living Christ appears a dogma to the Unitarian who feels he has got to something real in the Fatherhood of a personal God. Again, the conception of God as a Person is dogma from the standpoint represented by an eminent French Protestant, the late A. Sabatier. Yet to the Danish philosopher Höffding, who wrote a well-known book on the Philosophy of Religion, Sabatier does not seem radical enough. Sabatier still habitually uses phrases of God *as if* he were personal. We must give that up, Höffding says, and we shall touch ground at last in the bare belief

that the Universe is somehow of such a nature that
" values are conserved." But shall we ? Höffding's
optimistic supposition may seem a dogma to the man
who holds that we know absolutely nothing about the
Reality behind phenomena. Even here there is a possibility of dogma creeping in, if we are not careful. If we
assert definitely that the ground of the Universe is
unknowable, we still may be taxed with dogma by the
man who does not know enough about it even to say
whether in its essence it is unknowable or not, who will
go no further than to say that he personally does not
know. One sees that it is no simple matter to get rid
of Christian belief.

The Christian Church has suffered great changes in
the last half-century, but it has seen around it system
after system arise, have its day of vogue and pride, and
with strange rapidity sink into obsolescence. Spencer
and Haeckel, except for the less-cultured classes, are
gone ; Comtism is a thing of the past ; Pragmatism is
already *vieux jeu* ; Nietzsche from a prophet has become
an interesting literary phenomenon ; Bergson, whilst
hardly as yet an old man, has experienced the inevitable
reaction to the vehemence of his popular *réclame*. Whatever weaknesses the non-Christian world may discover
in Christianity, it has so far not been able in Europe to
put forward any rival theory of the Universe of equal
permanance and power. And one must notice how
much of the vague and informal religiosity which runs
through the modern world, far outside the confines of
the Christian Body, depends for its existence upon the
tradition of the Christian Church. It exhibits—to use
the figure of a philosophic observer, Ernst Troeltsch—

variations played by each virtuoso according to his individual fancy upon the Christian theme.

But if Christianity and non-Christian types of belief shade off into each other by all these gradations, it raises the question: What does one mean by Christianity? If one claims permanence for the Christian Church, in spite of the changes that have been admitted, one must indicate some essential thing which remains the same. The faith embodied in the Catholic creeds involves the belief that a Man who appeared among the Jews during the reign of the Emperor Tiberius and was executed by the Roman Government, as a nationalist pretender, stood to the Power governing the Universe in a relation so close that it can be described as personal identity. And it might seem that the formula " Jesus is God " gives a clear issue which would make a division between those who believe it and those who do not. If, however, we try to apply this as a criterion, we find that it is full of ambiguities. Even the orthodox Catholic theology does not assert that " God " and " Jesus " are coextensive. It allows that some propositions are true of Jesus which would not be true of God—that He " grew," for instance, " in wisdom and stature " ; and that some propositions are true of God which would not be true of Jesus—that He " so loved the world that He gave His only-begotten Son." The personal identity therefore asserted in the formula " Jesus is God " is not, according to the orthodox Catholic theology, the simple case of one individual denoted by two descriptions, as when one says " That man on the bay horse is the King of England." It is a case altogether unique and mysterious. The term " God " again has been used in a bewildering

number of senses ; according to some of these the formula
" Jesus is God " might mean nothing that was not true
of all good men—or of all men without distinction—or
of everything in the Universe.

The great dividing line, it appears to me, is that which
marks off all those who hold that the relation of Jesus
to God—however they describe or formulate it—is of
such a kind that it could not be repeated in any other
individual—that to speak in fact of its being repeated
in any *other* individual is a contradiction in terms, since
any individual standing in that relation to God would
be Jesus, and that Jesus, in virtue of this relation, has
the same absolute claim upon all men's worship and
loyalty as belongs to God. A persuasion of this sort of
uniqueness attaching to Jesus seems to me the essential
characteristic of what has actually in the field of human
history been Christianity.

This is the persuasion, with all that it implies, which
still animates the Christian Body and nerves it for
its tasks in the world. It cannot be denied that its
leaders have abandoned some of the beliefs attacked by
" Rationalists " two generations ago. If, however, any
enemy thinks that Christianity has thereby been brought
nearer to extinction, nearer to abandoning its central
and essential faith, the facts hardly seem to bear out
his assurance. It is important to realize that the abandoned beliefs belonged largely to a different category
from the beliefs retained. The abandoned beliefs related
to scientific and historical facts, and therefore brought
Christian tradition upon the territory claimed by Science
and History. Hence the conflict in a past generation
between " Moses and Geology," between tradition and

Hellenism and Christianity

Colenso. The beliefs retained relate to a region where neither Natural Science nor History, but only Philosophy, can exercise control. Whether the Ultimate Ground of the Universe is a Personal Will is not a question which we can settle by an appeal to visible or tangible facts. Any hypothesis as to the Ultimate Ground—the Christian's or the Agnostic's—makes no difference to Physics or Chemistry or Geology or Mathematics. The Christian belief, again, as to the significance of Jesus Christ rests upon certain value-judgements which objective History can no more prove or disprove than it can prove or disprove the value of a picture or of a sonata.

The effect of this change is that Christianity is no longer within grappling distance of its adversaries as in the old " Moses-and-Geology " days. Those were good old days for the " Rationalist " ; he could deal his blows with a light heart and feel them get home. It was an easy business which did not require much thought ; a brute fact or two lay always ready at hand to fling. We can understand that the " Rationalist " does not readily adjust himself to the new conditions. He can now close with Christianity only by rising to a region of systematic thought, where the " Rationalist " is not necessarily at home. And in the end you can never get a clear-cut, indubitable, matter-of-fact result, such as the old-fashioned " Rationalist " loved ! In the old days there seemed to be a certain number of facts, clearly established by Science, which stood in the way of Christian belief. There are none to-day—no facts, that is, except the great obvious fact of Evil, which is a difficulty, not for Christians only, but for any form of religious or optimistic belief—a moral, rather than a scientific, difficulty. One

Christianity in the Modern World

might describe the situation by saying that the obstructions which hindered the advance of the engine have been removed ; the track is clear ; if the engine does not move now, it is because the inner propelling power is wanting. It is not that the Christian hypothesis seems *impossible*, but that it seems *unnecessary*. All the difficulties which arise, as we saw, from Anthropology, from Philosophy, and from Psychology, act rather by weakening the motive power than by putting obstacles on the track. Very possibly this kind of difficulty is quite as serious, but it is certainly of a different kind.

But if Christian belief cannot be got at by any short knock-down argument, that means that it cannot be established either by argument of that kind. Argument, generally speaking, in religion, can do no more than clear the track ; it cannot make the engine move. One may, I think, divine that if the Christian Church is going to further its cause in the days to come, it will be by exhibiting a certain type of life realized in practice. An essential part of its case rests, as has been already said, upon judgements of value, where only individual perception, and not argument or scientific demonstration, can decide. The utmost that we can do to prove the value of a work of art to any other man is to call his attention to it. And if the Christian Church wants to convince the world of the supreme value of its ideal of love, it can only do so by steadily confronting the world with the actual thing. The real attraction to a society consists in what we call its special atmosphere. Supposing that the love which shines in certain individual Christian lives became general in the Christian society—a quickening of emotion and will which could be called love, not in any pale metaphorical sense, but in literal truth, a force shaping all conduct and social organization, heightening all life with an inexhaustible interest and energy—there would perhaps not be much need for books of Christian evidences. It is on the field of Philosophy, one may repeat, that the difficulties are found. And we may perhaps glance back at those indicated and see how such a realization of the Spirit of Christ would bear upon them.

There was the metaphysical theory which dissolved the unity of the individual person into a mental accompaniment of successive bodily states. It is in love that the consciousness of the unity of the person becomes most intense. Who loves a succession of mental states ?

There was the epistemological difficulty of faith and knowledge. To the lover it is not a paradox, but a truism, to say, " Blessed are they that have not seen and yet have believed."

There was the moral difficulty of God's forgiveness. In the life of love forgiveness is a matter of course.

There was the appearance of something unworthy in the relation of love between God and the human soul. It is only the full exhibition of what love is which can show its divine dignity.

There was the difficulty that the ethics of the Sermon on the Mount seemed servile. The lover, rejoicing in his service and sacrifice, could only laugh.

And, lastly, the Christian ideal seemed to imply an asceticism which diminished the personality and took

Christianity in the Modern World

the richness and the colour out of life. If the Christian ideal were realized, we should see so plainly the man who lost himself for Christ's sake find himself many times over, that to represent self-restraint by its negative side only would be an obvious foolishness.